T5-CSB-207

WITHDRAWN

LINGUISTICS IN REMEDIAL ENGLISH

JANUA LINGUARUM

STUDIA MEMORIAE
NICOLAI VAN WIJK DEDICATA

edenda curat

C. H. VAN SCHOONEVELD
INDIANA UNIVERSITY

SERIES PRACTICA
XLVII

1966
MOUTON & CO.
THE HAGUE · PARIS

LINGUISTICS
IN
REMEDIAL ENGLISH

by

JOHN C. FISHER

STATE UNIVERSITY COLLEGE, OSWEGO

1966

MOUTON & CO.

THE HAGUE · PARIS

Printed in The Netherlands.

to Warner G. Rice

PREFACE

Having taught the most frustrating of English courses, remedial composition, for several semesters with inadequate materials and methods, I began in 1960 to devise a course that would effectively change the language habits of students using nonstandard English. I decided to experiment with language learning procedures being utilized by teachers of English as a foreign language at the English Language Institute of the University of Michigan. My assumption was that since remedial students are learning a language that is foreign to them, modern methods of teaching languages can be used with profit.

In order to lessen the number of variables, I determined that I would teach only syntax and morphology by the methods of the English Language Institute. All other items such as punctuation, capitalization, and spelling would be taught conventionally, as they had been.

Because the lessons used at the English Language Institute were not adequate for the special problems of remedial students, it was necessary to isolate the grammatical errors of an experimental group of freshman students and to make a linguistic description of them. I then designed and used lessons based on the structural errors described. The experimental group met during the spring semester of 1961 at the State University College, Oswego, New York. The description of the errors and the results of using the lessons are found in the chapters that follow.

I must express my appreciation to the people who have contributed their time and energy to help further this research. My family, down to the smallest of them, assisted in various ways — some of them unbelievable. I am especially grateful to Albert H. Marckwardt for his encouragement when the project was forming, and to A. K. Stevens, Finley Carpenter, Harold King, Charles Kreidler, and Fred Walcott who read the manuscript and offered much-needed advice. For any errors in judgment that might appear, however, I am indebted only to myself. Finally, I give my thanks to the lesser heroes who made this book not only necessary but possible — my students.

Oswego, New York   J. C. F.
May 4, 1965

TABLE OF CONTENTS

PREFACE 7

I. THE PURPOSE OF THIS STUDY 13
   A. The Need for Research in Remedial English Composition 13
      1. The Colleges Requiring Remedial Composition 13
      2. The Inadequacy of Research 14
      3. The Inadequacy of Textual Materials and Techniques 15
   B. The Purpose of the Present Study 17
      1. The Isolation of Errors 17
      2. The Oral Pattern Practice Method 17
   C. The Limitations of This Study 19
   D. Summary 19

II. MAKING THE NEW PATTERNS HABITUAL 21
   A. A Definition of Habit 21
   B. The Difficulty of Changing Habits 21
   C. The Possibility of Making Correct Sentence Patterns Habitual . . . 22
      1. Isolating Errors 22
      2. Explaining the Rules of Syntax and Morphology 24
      3. The Reasons for Using an Oral Method 25
      4. The Reasons for Using a Pattern Practice Method 27
   D. Summary 29

III. METHODS USED IN THE ANALYSIS AND EXPERIMENT 30
   A. Isolating Subfreshman Students 30
   B. The Testing Program 30
      1. The Cooperative English Test 30
      2. The Subjective Grading of Final Papers 33
   C. Teaching at the Point of Error 33
   D. The Oral Pattern Practice Method 34
   E. The Writing of the Students 36
      1. Writing Restricted Patterns 36

2. Writing Themes   36
F. Summary   36

IV.   THE ANALYSIS OF ERRORS AND THE METHODS OF CORRECTION   37
A. The Matter of Usage   37
1. The Appeal to Linguistic Studies   37
2. Other Considerations   38
B. The Structures in Error   38
1. Verb Tense and Sequence   38
2. Run-On Sentences   40
3. Faulty Parallelism   41
4. Preposition and Sentence Group Modification   41
5. Sentence Fragments   42
6. Errors in the Plural   43
7. Errors in the Possessive   43
8. Lack of Pronoun Agreement   43
9. Adjective - Adverb   44
10. Subject-Verb Disagreement   44
11. Faulty Comparisons   45
12. A - An   46
C. Summary   46

V.   STATISTICAL FINDINGS   47
A. The Analysis of Errors   47
1. The Control Group   47
2. The Experimental Group   48
B. Findings of the Experiment   49
1. The Pre-Test Scores of the Control Group   49
2. The Pre-Test Scores of the Experimental Group   49
3. The Post-Test Scores of the Control Group   50
4. The Post-Test Scores of the Experimental Group   50
5. The Difference Between the Two Groups   50
6. The Relative Changes in Rank Order   51
7. The Results of the Subjective Test   51
C. Summary   51

VI.   RECOMMENDATIONS   53
A. Utilizing the Oral Pattern   53
B. Utilizing the Errors Described in Table 3   53
C. Making Grammatical Generalizations   53
D. Additional Needs   53
E. The Students' Ability to Do the Work   54

APPENDIX A 55

APPENDIX B 61

BIBLIOGRAPHY 70

I

THE PURPOSE OF THIS STUDY

A. THE NEED FOR RESEARCH IN REMEDIAL ENGLISH COMPOSITION

English teachers have long been concerned with the problem of dealing with students in need of remedial composition; and even with the changing complexion of our schools at all levels within recent years, the problem remains. In 1931, Leo Brueckner and Ernest Melby stated that their purpose in writing *Diagnostic and Remedial Teaching*, much of it concerned with composition, was "to assemble a body of material that will assist teachers and supervisors to reduce the amount of maladjustment in our schools..., and to increase the effectiveness with which the schools can deal with the individual differences of pupils".[1] In their book they are interested, in part, in techniques of instruction and in practical exercises "based in so far as possible on experimentation, that may be used to eliminate the faults revealed by the diagnostic study".[2] At least thirty years ago, then, students in need of remedial work were very much in evidence, and research was being conducted to lessen the problems in the schools.

1. *The Colleges Requiring Remedial Composition*

An overwhelming number of colleges and universities throughout the country offer evidence that the problem remains with us. According to Eldon Shupe's 1959 University of Michigan dissertation on remedial English at Flint Junior College, the data from four surveys conducted over a period of seven years indicate that one third of this country's institutions of higher education currently offer courses in remedial English.[3] One study made in 1957 informs us that reputable schools offer subfreshman courses in composition for an unusually large number of students. At Ohio State University, for instance, 33% of the freshmen were required to take remedial composition at the time of the survey. At Oklahoma A. and M. the figure was 30-40%.

---

[1] Leo J. Brueckner and Ernest O. Melby, *Diagnostic and Remedial Teaching* (Boston, Houghton Mifflin Co., 1931), p. 11.
[2] *Ibid.*, p. 14.
[3] Eldon E. Shupe, Jr., "An Evaluation of Remedial English at Flint Junior College". Unpublished Ed. D. in English dissertation, Dept. of English, University of Michigan (1959), p. 3.

The number reached 65% at the lesser-known Valdosta State College.[4] The numbers suggest that the subfreshman course has not seen its day and is not likely to for some time, even though there are indications that colleges have become less interested in it within the past few years.

2. *The Inadequacy of Research*

One would assume that a problem as great as this would result in up-to-date literature designed to lessen it. But such has not been the case. There have been no recent valid analyses of students' writing abnormalities and no pedagogical techniques or textbooks. For several reasons the analyses of student errors we have before us are invalid for the college student in need of remedial work. They are often based on the study of oral language; not only are they reports of elementary and secondary grades, but they are vague; and attitudes toward language have changed since the most popular error counts were compiled.

A speech error will occur in a student's writing — indeed, much of the present work is predicated on that assumption — but a person reporting speech errors is unable to make an adequate report of all errors that occur. Martin Stormzand and M. V. O'Shea, reporting an error count, maintained "it is obvious that children, in talking, confuse dependent and independent clauses, but no such errors were reported by the teachers, who, intent upon errors in the use of parts of speech..., paid little attention to the longer clauses".[5] They go on to say that unless faults in sentence structure are especially flagrant they will command attention only when they are seen in print. It takes time for an investigator to locate most errors and isolate them by type, and that time does not exist if he records words while they are being spoken. And some errors, such as run-on sentences and fragments, must be written in order to be located at all.

An investigation of oral errors reported by teachers was made by W. W. Charters and Edith Miller in Kansas City, Missouri, in 1915, for elementary school children, not for college students.[6] Other investigators made similar error counts based on the same classification of oral errors, and a "common error" list was compiled by R. L. Lyman, who found a striking similarity in the types of errors found in six studies: verb forms, 49-62%; syntactical redundancy, 9-21%; pronouns, 10-14%; double negatives, 8-14%.[7] Not quite so incomplete but almost as vague is Pressey's 1925 study which listed errors only under the headings, "Fragments", "Stringy Sentences", "Choppy Sentences", "Parallelism", "Pronoun with no Antecedent", "Pronoun not

---

[4] "Has English Zero Seen Its Day? — A Symposium", *College Composition and Communication*, VIII (May, 1957), pp. 72-95.

[5] Martin J. Stormzand and M. V. O'Shea, *How Much English Grammar?* (Baltimore, Warwick and York, Inc., 1924), p. 184.

[6] W. W. Charters and Edith Miller, *A Course of Study in Grammar*, Vol. 16, University of Missouri Bulletin, Education Series 9 (Columbia, Miss., University of Missouri, January, 1915).

[7] Rollo LaVerne Lyman, *Summary of Investigations Relating to Grammar, Language and Composition* (Supplementary Educational Monographs) (Chicago, University of Chicago, 1929).

near Antecedent", "Change in Tense", "Redundancy and Repetition", "Omitted Word or Phrase", "Incoherent Sentence", and "Miscellaneous".[8] There is little or no attempt in these studies to break down the errors within each classification. One wonders which verb forms, for instance, were in error. An incoherent sentence may lack clarity for any one of a number of reasons. There could be an error in diction, or a faulty comparison. In order to prevent the error from recurring, the teacher must have a closer analysis of the type. A diction problem must be treated differently from a structure problem such as a faulty comparison.

3. *The Inadequacy of Textual Materials and Techniques*

This vagueness appears not only in the records of students' errors, but also in the materials designed to lessen the errors. Brueckner and Melby advise that:

study helps to guide the pupils over known crucial steps in the learning process reduce the likelihood of failure to master the step. ... The use of charts and other means of helping the pupil to visualize correct forms..., and to determine the nature and causes of deviations from satisfactory standards is a direct contribution to teaching that grew out of the attempts to study the classroom product objectively.[9]

There are no study helps or charts offered by Brueckner and Melby, however, that will help the student attain the satisfactory standards about which they speak. Lyman states that class time may be used profitably for drilling both individuals and groups, and for laboratory procedures,[10] but he provides no lessons that will make the class and laboratory profitable. The maxims of H. J. Arnold offer no technique specific enough to take into the classroom, in spite of his title, "Diagnostic and Remedial Techniques for College Freshmen". He suggests that teachers of remedial English should use self-taught practice exercises and help their students attain "definite abilities, first by teaching and then by providing sufficient practice to fix the response in the student's mind".[11] There is no indication, however, of the form the practice exercises or the teaching are to take.

The colleges themselves, even after struggling with the problem first hand for years, seem to have no technique. Each instructor teaches the course as he sees fit, with only the barest of advice from his department. The syllabus at Stanford University states that English R, the remedial course, should be "basically a review course in fundamentals of current usage, syntax, grammar, punctuation and spelling".[12] As Shupe says: "It is readily apparent from the writing that there is considerable variance among colleges and universities as to what they consider remedial English courses to be, and

[8] S. L. Pressey, "A Statistical Study of Children's Errors in Sentence Structure", *English Journal*, Vol. 14 (September, 1925), pp. 529-35.
[9] Brueckner and Melby, *op. cit.*, p. 14.
[10] Lyman, *op. cit.*, pp. 253-255.
[11] H. J. Arnold, "Diagnostic and Remedial Techniques for College Freshmen", *Association of American Colleges Bulletin*, Vol. 16 (1930), p. 268.
[12] Syllabus entitled "Instructor's Guide for English R", cited by Shupe, *op. cit.*, p. 7.

what approaches they think should be taken in teaching these courses."[13] There seems, then, to be no general trend regarding these matters.

Two of the traditional methods of teaching freshman composition have also been used for remedial students in subfreshman courses. One method is to utilize workbooks in which the student fills in blank spaces and rewrites sentences. The other method is to review rules of grammar and offer the student writing experiences that should make use of the rules. There are valid reasons for discouraging these methods. Robert Pooley contends that while workbook practice may give the brighter pupil the opportunity to discover subtleties of the language, it may give the slower pupil only the opportunity to reinforce bad habits because he will be likely to supply a form that is familiar to him. Pooley goes on to say that "usage practice must be heard and spoken to be effective".[14] Another point that can be made is that the workbook does not present a lifelike situation to the student, and so it is likely to provide little transfer of training from the exercise to his writing. When a person writes he structures words into sentences; he does not fit words into the blank spaces of already completed sentences.

The grammatical method, widespread as it is, seems even less effective than that of the workbook. Most teachers in this writer's experience, and many who have been influenced by recent language study, are convinced that there is little relation between a student's ability to classify sentences and his ability to apply the knowledge to better his writing. The study of grammar, like the use of the workbook, is more likely to prove useful to the more able student, not to the less able one:

The students who have the most trouble using English are those who find systematic grammar too difficult to learn even though a very gradual and concrete approach is maintained. The slower a student is, therefore, the less reliance should be put on grammatical generalizations and classifications as a means of improving his understanding or use of English. He is likely to profit more from direct teaching and habit formation of a particular detail of good usage.[15]

One reason for this statement by the Commission on the English Curriculum of the National Council of Teachers of English is that courses of study abound in definitions which are likely to confuse the average student and which are certain to confuse the remedial one. He readily gives up when faced with such terms as *predicate, transitive verb, copulative verb, subjective complement, adjective clause, adverb,* and *adverbial clause.*

Another reason for the above statement by the Commission is that the traditional analysis of English is suspect. Earlier in their report the Commission stated that, "for more than a generation, linguistic scholars have been examining critically the

---

[13]   *Ibid.*
[14]   Robert C. Pooley, *Teaching English Usage* (New York, C. Appleton-Century Co., Inc., 1946), p. 184.
[15]   The Commission on the English Curriculum of the National Council of Teachers of English, *The English Language Arts in the Secondary School* (New York, Appleton-Century- Crofts, Inc., 1956), p. 368.

shortcomings of the present system of analysis, which was organized in the eighteenth century by analogy with the grammar of Latin...".[16] They went on to say that, "the teacher of English who is honestly trying to do his best possible teaching of grammar ... cannot rely securely on the grammatical analysis which he was probably taught...".[17] This implies that an eighteenth-century analysis by its nature cannot take into account the fact that language changes and in fact has changed in the past two hundred years.

The teacher of remedial composition, however, has to realize that language changes. He is continually faced with an emergency situation. Even if an eighteenth-century style were desirable, he must grapple with flagrant and persistent errors, such as fragments and run-on sentences, some of which were acceptable in the eighteenth century. It is these flagrant and persistent errors, not the niceties of style, to which the teacher must direct his attention.

B. THE PURPOSE OF THE PRESENT STUDY

1. *The Isolation of Errors*

Because the traditional workbook and grammatical methods had not proved to be satisfactory in teaching remedial composition to a control group at the State University College at Oswego, New York, and because no adequate materials were available, the present writer set about to devise materials and a method that would be effective. It seemed logical that he should first determine what errors his students from all areas of New York State were making, then devise lessons based not only on the errors but also on a suitable teaching method, and, finally, use the lessons. The errors were analyzed on modern linguistic principles. The method decided upon and used with an experimental group was the oral pattern practice approach used by the writer in teaching English as a foreign language at the English Language Institute of the University of Michigan. The method has had good results in teaching a foreign language quickly, and although none of the textbooks with which this writer was familiar utilized the method for teaching a native language, it was hypothesized by this writer that it would work just as well with students whose native language at times seemed to be foreign to them.

2. *The Oral Pattern Practice Method*

C. C. Fries, the founder of the English Language Institute, defines *oral approach* as "a name primarily for the end to be attained in the first stage of language learning rather than a descriptive limitation of the permissible devices to attain the end. The end is the building up of a set of habits for the oral production of a language."[18] In

---

[16] *Ibid.*, p. 356.
[17] *Ibid.*
[18] C. C. Fries, *Teaching and Learning English as a Foreign Language* (Ann Arbor, University of Michigan Press, 1945), p. 8.

this work, however, the term has a less restrictive meaning. It describes the means by which the end is attained, as well as the end itself.

It was decided that the students were to practice English sentence patterns orally by repeating, substituting, and transforming them in the manner of the lessons in grammar taught at the English Language Institute. They would orally repeat a series of sentences after the instructor, or substitute a word or a group of words to make an otherwise identical sentence, or convert one or two sentences into another according to some plan directed by the instructor. Although a language response differs in each situation that occurs, standard patterns of the language remain generally fixed, and can be taught as units. Otto Jesperson says that:

> free expressions ... have to be treated in each case anew by the speaker, who inserts the words that fit the particular situation. The sentence he thus creates may, or may not, be different in some one or more respects from anything he has ever heard or uttered before ... [but] in pronouncing it he conforms to a certain pattern. No matter what words he inserts, he builds up the sentence in the same way, and even without special grammatical training we feel that the two sentences
> John gave Mary the apple,
> My uncle lent the joiner five shillings
> are analogous, that is, they are made after the same pattern. ... The words that make up the sentences are variable, but the type is fixed.[19]

These types, the patterns, are what the students in need of remedial work must be taught, because it is the types which are in error in their writing.

The exercises in repetition, substitution, and transformation, it was hypothesized, would teach the students the language patterns about which Jespersen writes. The students would first orally repeat a series of structurally identical sentences after the teacher, observing the structure so that they could later generalize about the grammatical principles involved. For instance, after repeating a series of sentences such as those given to us above by Jespersen, the students might comment about the relative positions of subject, verb, "receiver of action", and "the thing received". In order to reinforce the pattern and make it automatic, this writer decided to make the students then substitute within the pattern, or frame. In Jespersen's examples the frame is, of course, subject, verb, indirect object, direct object. They would be told to repeat the original sentence, "John gave Mary the apple", and then instructed to substitute the word "car" in the appropriate place, with the result, "John gave Mary the car", supplied by the students. Given the word "bicycle", the sentence would be pronounced, "John gave Mary the bicycle". If the next word supplied were "sent", the students would say, "John sent Mary the bicycle." In the transformation exercises, one or two sentences would be transformed into another pattern requested by the teacher. If he were to request a pattern like Jespersen's, he might say, "The apple was given to Mary by John", "John gave the apple to Mary", or, "John gave it to Mary. It was an apple", with the students' rejoinder, "John gave Mary the apple." There is a fuller

[19]   Otto Jespersen, *The Philosophy of Grammar* (London, George Allen and Unwin, Ltd., 1924), p. 19.

demonstration of repetition, substitution and transformation in Chapter III where the experimental method used here is described in detail.

Only after the patterns were fixed by the oral method would the students write, and then they would first write the patterns they had already practiced orally. At the close of each class session the students were to be given copies of the lessons they had just completed. The substitution and transformation exercises were to be written out and given to the instructor at the next class meeting.

C. THE LIMITATIONS OF THIS STUDY

The analysis of errors, the materials, and the instruction were to be limited to syntax and morphology, and errors that could be remedied by snytax and morphology lessons. On the basis of his experience in teaching English as a foreign language, this writer felt that the oral pattern practice approach was best suited to teach patterns of phrase and word structure. According to Pooley, syntax includes subject-verb agreement, pronoun agreement, adverbial modification, double negatives, dangling modifiers, noun or pronoun with gerund, and comparison of adjectives. Morphology includes verb forms, adjective-adverb, and noun and pronoun cases.[20]

In order to determine whether or not the oral pattern practice approach would prove to be effective after analyzing errors, it was decided to compare it with the more traditional approach dictated by conventional textbooks. The results of this comparison between Group E, the experimental group using textual material devised by this writer, and Group C, the control group using traditional material, will be found in Chapter V.

D. SUMMARY

Remedial English composition has long been the concern of educators at all levels, and if the number of remedial courses being offered at the present time in the colleges and universities of this country is any indication, it will be the concern of educators for a long time to come. One would suspect, then, that the syntax and morphology problems of students needing remedial work would long have been the object of research, and that textual materials based on the findings of the research would have been written. What research work that has been done, however, is not recent and is of little use, at least to college instructors who teach remedial composition. The error counts are based mostly on speech, rather than on writing, and when they are at all complete, they are complete only for the elementary or lower secondary grades.

Materials that have philosophized about remedial problems have been too vague to prescribe any specific methods by which a teacher of remedial English might lessen the number of errors his students make in their writing. The methods that have been

---

[20] Pooley, *op. cit., passim.*

used are generally the same as those used to teach students in regular composition sections. That is, either a workbook or a traditional textbook forms the basis for a studial approach with the expectation that required compositions will help the students make use of the rules they have "learned" in class.

Because there have been no satisfactory descriptions of the syntax and morphology constructions of remedial college students, and no satisfactory materials designed to remedy their nonstandard constructions, the present writer decided to analyze errors and devise lessons. It was his hypothesis that after making a descriptive analysis of students' errors he could use the analysis as a basis for oral pattern practice lessons similar to those used to teach English as a foreign language at the English Language Institute of the University of Michigan.

II

MAKING THE NEW PATTERNS HABITUAL

The basic problem in teaching grammar to any composition student, whether in a regular or a remedial section, is to find the best means by which the training he receives in class may be transferred to his written work. The class work, at least of the student who repeatedly writes nonstandard English constructions, must be made habit, that is, automatic, in order to effect this transfer. That is an extremely difficult thing to do, of course, because the nonstandard structures of the student are already habitual. These poor habits are deeply ingrained because the student has had them for years.

Remedial students, however, will make grammatically correct sentences automatic if the teacher will first isolate the errors of his students, then make them generalize about a construction they have repeated after him, and finally use an oral pattern practice method.

A. A DEFINITION OF HABIT

A habit is generally understood to be a regularly occurring, inevitable response to a particular complex stimulus. But that definition is not necessarily true. Knight Dunlap tells us that "in many cases ... no such stereotype of action can be discerned. One may progressively change the performance, continuously varying it, while constantly learning."[1] Only a part of the complex stimulus needs to be recognized in order to bring about the complete reaction previously made only to the whole. A pattern tends to recur when only a part of it is stimulated.[2]

B. THE DIFFICULTY OF CHANGING HABITS

One can justifiably ask if a person needing remedial work can change from his already acquired undesirable habits to new desirable ones. Recognizing that language learning is a process of habit-forming, Harold Palmer doubts that a person can ever observe,

[1] Knight Dunlap, *Habits, Their Making and Unmaking* (New York, Liveright, Inc., 1932), p. 8.
[2] H. L. Hollingworth, *The Psychology of Thought* (New York, D. Appleton-Century Co., 1926), p. 94.

reproduce and imitate accurately unless he does so in the elementary stages of his language study.[3]

C. THE POSSIBILITY OF MAKING CORRECT SENTENCE PATTERNS HABITUAL

The remedial student in a college class is certainly not in the elementary stages of his language study, even though he needs work in the fundamentals of the language. Apparently, however, school administrators, heads of English departments, and teachers throughout the country believe, for one reason or another, that a person's habits can be changed. The evidence in Chapter I is indication enough that a whole system of subfreshman, and indeed freshman, composition teaching is predicated on the belief that errors can be eliminated, and that students can substitute one set of habits for another. As William James has noted,

the habits of an elementary particle of matter cannot change (on the principle of the atomistic philosophy), because the particle is itself an unchangeable thing; but those of a compound mass of matter can change, because they are ... due to the structure of the compound, and either outward forces or inward tensions can ... turn the structure into something different from what it was.[4]

Language is structured into sentences, and so it seems reasonable to assume that the habits of students, even those in need of remedial work, can be changed. The question remains, however, how best to bring about the change.

1. *Isolating Errors*

There is no sense in a teacher's attempting to change habits that are already normal, so he must inevitably isolate the errors of his students, even if he only corrects their papers and offers his comments. When he corrects a specific error he is, in effect, isolating it from all other possible errors and calling the student's attention only to a structure that causes him trouble. This has the beneficial effect of teaching the student only those things he needs to be taught. Too often, however, the teacher undoes this effect by teaching items in class that would infrequently or never be in error in actual use. Stormzand and O'Shea have said that verbs need to be dealt with extensively in a grammar course because they are so complex, but some forms need be treated only summarily if one gives regard to "infrequent usage".[5] This writer will go a step further than Stormzand and O'Shea by stating that with remedial students it is unnecessary even to mention a form unless it is misused. There are constructions enough that are nonstandard, each one presenting a major problem to the student in need of remedial

---

[3] Harold E. Palmer, *The Principles of Language Study* (London, George G. Harrap and Co., Ltd., 1921), p. 17.
[4] William James, *The Principles of Psychology*, Vol. I (New York, Henry Holt and Co., 1890), p. 104.
[5] Stormzand and O'Shea, *op. cit.*, p. 135.

work. The number of items to be studied must be limited so as to teach only that which is most needed. If they did nothing else, the Charters-Miller and other studies of error frequency showed that only a few critical forms need extensive work. In this area we can learn from the teachers of English as a foreign language. The teacher of a second language must compare the structures of the native language and of the one to be learned in order to discover what differences there are. It is the difference in structure that the student is taught. It is possible, also, to base a course in remedial English on those points of difference between the nonstandard structures of the students and the standard structures of English. It was the task of this writer to find the nonstandard grammatical structures in the writing of the remedial students he intended to teach by the experimental pattern practice approach. This was done by analyzing the sentence structures in ten thousand words written by the experimental group of twenty-two students during the first week of the semester in which they were taught.

When an investigator isolates errors and determines their frequencies he can offer more than individual instruction. If his investigation has been extensive he can offer a complete course of instruction for the kind of student about whose writing he has gathered data. If he has gathered data from the writing of all his students in a particular class, his findings can be used as a basis for teaching by group instruction as well as by individual instruction. Class time is most profitably used by teaching to the whole class, rather than to individuals. Lyman suggests that frequent errors be attended to by a group of students, while infrequent errors be attended to by individuals.[6] Glenn M. Blair, writing directly to teachers of remedial students, states:

Every teacher of remedial English might well conduct ... a study in his own classes in an effort to discover the characteristic errors of his pupils. The data obtained from such a survey can be used to good advantage in planning the program of instruction. Errors common to large numbers of pupils can be handled in group fashion while those errors causing trouble to relatively few pupils can be handled on an individual basis.[7]

If a student is aware that he, or at the very least his group, needs the instruction being given in class, he is more likely to be kindly disposed to it. It is only natural that a kind disposition toward material to be learned will make that material easier to learn. A course based to a great extent on frequency of error and completely on demonstrated error will give him the awareness he needs. The Commission on the English Curriculum has commented that

the teaching of English should be in relation to ... [the student's] need for understanding and using this particular point in connection with his own problems. ... There is far more chance of teaching a grammatical point ... in such a way that the student will actually learn it and use it effectively, if it is taught when he has demonstrated a real need for it.[8]

---

[6]   Lyman, *op. cit.*, p. 75.
[7]   Glenn Myers Blair, *Diagnostic and Remedial Teaching in Secondary Schools* (New York, The Macmillan Co., 1946), p. 345.
[8]   The Commission on the English Curriculum, *op. cit.*, p. 367.

If the teacher has recorded errors and the frequencies with which they occur, the student has tangible evidence, and usually a great deal of it, that he is in need of the specific lesson he is going to study that day. This is evidence that the teacher can lay before the student before they begin to work. Too often, several weeks of a semester have elapsed before a student has written enough to demonstrate to himself a need for the work he has been doing. These weeks to some extent, then, are lost to him.

2. *Explaining the Rules of Syntax and Morphology*

There are discussions for and against explaining rules of syntax and morphology to composition students, including those who need a remedial course. No one seems adamant in the opinion that either the conscious or the subconscious method is better for the student who needs his writing habits greatly remedied. Palmer feels that a course for such a student should be a corrective one that would attempt to replace unsound methods and material by sound methods and material. The student must be taught a new language and it must be taught by utilizing only a spontaneous method.[9] Palmer writes of foreign language study, but his theory, if it is sound at all, is sound also for native language study. It seems reasonable to assume that a person who needs his habits changed in his native language is in no better circumstances than a person who needs them changed in a foreign language. The comments of Fries, although directed toward teachers of a foreign language — this time English as a foreign language — seem appropriate for the teacher of the remedial student. He reminds us that the child learning his own language does not merely repeat what he hears. Rather, he learns the "form and arrangement" of utterances and he then fits various words into them. These patterns, or frames, he contends, are the grammar and are to be learned by the child if he is to use the language. If the adult has not made the necessary forms habitual he can be helped considerably by someone who generalizes about the forms with which he has difficulty.[10] Fries does not at all suggest, however, that generalizing should play a major role in teaching new structures.

Although Palmer thinks that the adult can be helped by general statements, he is entirely at issue with those people who maintain that a studial or explanatory method is indispensable in memorizing and in making new patterns habitual. Nor does he agree with those who claim to be unable to memorize what they cannot understand. He argues that successful linguists, and here the term means "polyglots", have memorized sentences they could not analyze.[11] He also says:

Language study is essentially a habit-forming process. We speak and understand automatically as a result of perfectly formed habits. No foreign word or sentence is really 'known' until the student can produce it automatically (i.e. without hesitation or conscious calculation). Most of the time spent by the teacher in demonstrating why a ... sentence is constructed in a particular way is time wasted; it is generally enough for the student to learn to do things

---

[9]   Palmer, *The Principles of Language Study*, p. 55.
[10]   Fries, *Teaching and Learning English as a Foreign Language*, pp. 28-29.
[11]   Palmer, *The Principles of Language Study*, pp. 102-103.

without learning why he must do them (due exception being made in special cases, notably that of corrective courses).[12]

This suggests, then, that while the subconscious method alone may be advantageous to the average person, the remedial student will need the studial method in addition, although it should not assume a place of major importance. Perhaps the most significant statement on the subject has come from the National Council of Teachers of English commission which suggests that the student develop clear concepts by finding for himself the principle that governs a number of carefully prepared sentences presented by the teacher.[13] This is the technique used by the English Language Institute in its grammar textbook, *English Sentence Patterns*, especially designed for making English structures habitual for foreign students of the language.[14] It is the technique used in the experiment described in this work. The student listens to the teacher and repeats a series of sentences that are structurally similar, after being asked to observe the position or use of a word or group of words. When this exercise in repetition is completed, the student is expected to generalize about those structures to which his attention has been called.

3. *The Reasons for Using an Oral Method*

In order to make a new language, or a new dialect of a native language, automatic, an oral pattern practice approach, one that forces the student to respond orally in a prescribed pattern, will do at least as well for the student's sentence structure as writing will, and possibly even better. Quite a number of linguists tell us that written language is merely a symbol, and not a very accurate one, for spoken language. One of the most notable of these is Fries who claims that "the speech *is* the language".[15] Writing has represented language for only a fraction of the number of centuries that man has been speaking. What we attempt to do when we write is to capture as well as we possibly can the thoughts already formed in our minds. Those thoughts are transformed into speech and it is this speech that we transfer to paper when we write. What our students write, then, they first articulate. Palmer describes the process as "inner-articulating" and he writes of it:

We articulate mentally [while] our speech muscles, without necessarily moving, are stimulated by the nerves communicating with the speech-centre of our brain. Articulation in some form or other is the indispensable and invariable concomitant of memorizing speech-material. ... Words and word-groups are not perceived by the normal language user so long as they have not produced some sort of reaction in his vocal apparatus.[16]

---

[12] *Ibid.*, p. 21.
[13] The Commission on the English Curriculum, *op. cit.*, p. 377.
[14] English Language Institute Staff, *English Sentence Patterns* (Ann Arbor, University of Michigan Press, 1960).
[15] Fries, *Teaching and Learning English as a Foreign Language*, p. 6.
[16] Harold E. Palmer, *The Oral Method of Teaching Languages* (Cambridge, W. Heffer and Sons Ltd., 1923), pp. 21-22.

The oral approach, then, is the natural approach. If articulation is already one of the habits of the student, it seems likely that a method utilizing articulation would be highly efficient.

It is likely that a poor writer speaks badly also. Charters and Miller realized this when they found that all classes of oral errors appeared in lists of students' written errors. Therefore, it is reasonable to assume that if a person's oral language is restructured, there will be a decided effect on his written language. And Palmer, again, tells us that the oral course can play a great role in correcting poor language habits. One method of acquiring speech material is to observe someone articulate correctly, not only for sound but for structure, and to repeat either immediately or a long time later.[17] The student should use his ears before his eyes, receive before he produces, repeat orally before he reads, repeat in chorus before he repeats individually, and do drill work before free work.[18] Repetition exercises at the beginning of each of the lessons devised by this writer are designed to give the student the opportunity to hear and repeat in chorus before he responds individually.

Although Palmer's suggestions are made for students of a foreign language, they are principles that the present writer has followed for students needing remedial work. As a teacher of both English as a foreign language and remedial English, he is convinced that the difference between the two kinds of students is not so remote as one might think. There is a striking parallel between the problems in English as a foreign language, and those in the subfreshman composition course. Fries tells us that the process of acquiring a new social dialect of a native language has much in common with the process of learning a foreign language.[19] This is the attitude, also, of the authors of a symposium sponsored several years ago by the Conference on College Composition and Communication, entitled "English as a Second Language — Potential Applications to Teaching the Freshman Course". According to one of the authors, Robert Lado, the dialect styles of students

may be likened to the native language of the foreign students. ... The task of the teacher then is to give the student the use of other dialects and styles he will need for communication. ... The student's use of his native dialects and styles is anchored on firmly established systems of habits, and as in foreign language learning, we can assume that in spite of himself he will transfer those habits to the new dialect and styles he is trying to learn. ... In order for the student to have at his command the new resources of the language, he will have to acquire new sets of habits.[20]

Those new habits, as Lado goes on to tell us, can be acquired with the oral approach.

The oral approach offers the student the opportunity to react immediately and often

---

[17] *Ibid.*, p. 23.
[18] Palmer, *The Principles of Language Study*, p. 23.
[19] C. C. Fries, *The Teaching of the English Language* (New York, Thomas Nelson and Sons, 1927), p. 144.
[20] Robert Lado, "Sentence Structure", *College Composition and Communication*, VIII (February, 1957), pp. 14-15.

to new patterns to which he has just been exposed. William James has this to say about verbal response:

No reception without reaction, no impression without correlative expression, — this is the great maxim which the teacher ought never to forget.

An impression which simply flows in at the pupil's eyes or ears, and in no way modifies his active life, is an impression gone to waste. It is physiologically incomplete. It leaves no fruits behind it in the way of capacity acquired. Even as mere impression, it fails to produce its proper effect upon the memory. ... Its *motor consequences* are what clinch it. Some effect due to it in the way of an activity must return to the mind in the form of the *sensation of having acted*, and connect itself with the impression. The most durable impressions are those on account of which we speak or act, or else are inwardly convulsed.

The older pedagogic method of learning things by rote, and reciting them parrot-like in the schoolroom, rested on the truth that a thing merely read or heard, and never verbally reproduced, contracts the weakest possible adhesion of the mind. Verbal recitation or reproduction is thus a highly important kind of reactive behavior on our impressions. ...[21]

4. *The Reasons for Using a Pattern Practice Method*

In the oral pattern practice approach, the student verbally recites his lessons. James' comments, of course, do not exclude writing as an essential in making a new pattern habitual. An oral pattern practice approach, however, more efficiently evokes an immediate response on the part of the student. With its repeated recitations of structural patterns it is, as Fries claims, a more economical way to reinforce and make structures automatic than any other.[22] Each student can recite more quickly than he can write, and as a student repeats a pattern in imitation of the teacher, substitutes one pattern for another, or transforms one or two patterns into another, each of the other students can determine the proper response for himself. When the class recites in chorus, each student is forced to respond aloud more often than he does in a class using conventional methods.

Because language learning is such a problem for the remedial student, there should be a minimum number of usable patterns for him to make habitual. This kind of student will only be confused if he is taught a variety of constructions that are possible in a particular situation. What grammar he is taught should be accurate, but not complete. One or two all-inclusive patterns that he can remember will serve him better than a number of patterns he is likely to forget. It is in the repetition of a minimum number of patterns that the student makes a new language automatic. If the student is given a language situation to which he must respond immediately and often, the reaction will eventually become automatic — that is, without conscious thought. This is habit. But as Fries says, there must be repeated practice of the same patterns with varied content before the patterns themselves become automatic.[23] This repeated practice would satisfy Blair, who asks teachers of remedial English to

---

[21] William James, *Talks to Teachers on Psychology* (New York, Henry Holt and Co., 1939), pp. 33-34.
[22] Fries, *Teaching and Learning English as a Foreign Language*, p. 6.
[23] *Ibid.*, p. 9.

provide opportunities for their students to use the forms they are learning. He cautions that "the chief cause of deficiency in oral and written expression is probably *lack of experience and practice in using correct forms*".[24] Blair recognizes that a student who sits in a class where patterns are discussed, but not immediately used, does not necessarily use those patterns later when he writes his papers.

When the student imitates or repeats the pattern of the teacher, he is learning language naturally. Jespersen has said that, "as a bright contrast to the 'constructive' method of procedure, we have the 'imitative' method, which may be so called partly because it is an imitation of the way in which a child learns his native language, partly because it depends upon that invaluable faculty, the natural imitative instinct of the pupils, to give them the proper linguistic feeling".[25] It seems likely that any material fitted to a natural learning process would be learned easily.

One of the most frequently stated objections to imitation is that it does not allow the student to develop a style of his own. The person who makes this comment, however, is not speaking about the remedial student whose least important problem has to do with the niceties of style. If syntax and morphology are considered to be matters of style, then one can conclude that the remedial student has already proven his inability to develop an acceptable style on his own. No one need be overly concerned, then, if a teacher deliberately proceeds to change it.

At the beginning of this chapter, it was suggested that habit is not necessarily a regularly occurring response. There does not have to be a stereotype of action. The response may progressively vary. Such is the case when the technique of substitution is used during pattern practice exercises. The student's oral response is predetermined, but he must substitute a word or group of words for another in a structure given him by the instructor. The class is given a model sentence, such as "He works easily", and is told to substitute in the same frame. When the teacher pronounces the word "quickly", the class replies "He works quickly". If the teacher next pronounces "ran", the class replies "He ran quickly". The response progressively varies because in successive sentences the change can be in the subject, verb, preposition or sentence group, or any one of a number of other units of structure being taught. This work reinforces the student's conscious knowledge of word and group positions, but more than that it forces him to grope so quickly and often for correct responses that the knowledge enters his subconscious and becomes automatic; that is, a matter of habit.

Transformation exercises go beyond the repetition and substitution exercises by more closely approaching the natural situation that faces man each time he wants to express an experience with language. When man experiences he must synthesize the elements of the experience into one of a number of sentence patterns and fit the vocabulary dictated by the situation into the pattern. The experience is given to the students by the instructor, but they must synthesize, or transform, it into a sentence pattern to which

[24]   Blair, *op. cit.*, p. 355.
[25]   Otto Jespersen, *How to Teach a Foreign Language* (London, S. Sonnenschein Co., Ltd., 1904), p. 124.

they are arbitrarily limited by the instructor. The arbitrary limitation is invoked, of course, in order to facilitate learning. If students had a wide number of choices none could become automatic in a short space of time. After repeating and substituting in a number of sentences identical in pattern to "He works easily", the teacher might supply the sentences, "She wept. She could not be controlled." The oral response of the class would be "She wept uncontrollably." Stormzand and O'Shea suggest that teaching methods be worked out that will provide students with the opportunity to write and speak correct and varied sentence patterns. They think that two approaches seem possible: "— either to lead the pupil to think so as to compel such expression, or to require him to re-think and re-express thoughts presented to him in a form that shall be suitable for restatement involving practice in the forms desired."[26] Transformation exercises, of course, are designed to make the student re-think and re-express his thoughts in a suitable form. The student combines the elements of two simple phrases, clauses, or sentences into a more complex structure. The transfer of training is inevitable, since, when we write, there occur in our minds sentence elements which we must put together.

D. SUMMARY

In order for remedial composition teaching to be effective, the new syntax and morphology patterns the student studies in class must be made habitual. This does not mean that the same response must occur in all situations, but that the same frame or pattern must occur in which the student can fit the vocabulary for the particular response he needs.

The teacher of remedial English can learn from the teachers of English as a foreign language how to determine what patterns or frames he should teach. He should compare the grammar structures of his students with the structures of standard English, and at those points where they differ he will find the material upon which to design his course.

The next problem for the teacher is to determine which method of correction will best make the new patterns habitual. This writer decided that the oral pattern practice approach as developed by the English Language Institute to teach English as a foreign language is, theoretically, an acceptable method of teaching composition to remedial students, even though it was not designed specifically for that purpose. These two kinds of students have parallel problems because each is, in essence, learning a new language. With this approach the students have the opportunity to react immediately and efficiently to new patterns, and this is essential in making them habitual. The oral pattern practice approach makes use of repetition, substitution and transformation exercises which are a natural and efficient method of making correct sentence patterns automatic.

[26] Stormzand and O'Shea, *op. cit.*, p. 31.

III

METHODS USED IN THE ANALYSIS AND EXPERIMENT

A. ISOLATING SUBFRESHMAN STUDENTS

The problem of determining whether a student needs subfreshman work in English composition has not been satisfactorily solved, nor will it be solved in these pages. For the purpose of this study it was arbitrarily decided that a freshman at the State University College at Oswego, New York, who had an entrance score below 50.0 on the American Council on Education's Cooperative English Test, Mechanics of Expression, would be a candidate for remedial work. A score of 50.0, according to the norms for public secondary schools of the East, Middle West, and West, places a student slightly below the eleventh grade mean of 50.5, or slightly more than two grades below college level.

At the beginning of the spring semester of 1958, thirteen students were assigned to a remedial section of freshman composition at the State University College at Oswego, New York. They were placed in the section because their scores on the Cooperative English Test, Mechanics of Expression, had been below 50.0. Another student volunteered to take the course, which brought the total to fourteen. This group was taught conventionally with a traditional textbook and so became the control group, Group C, for the experiment described here. At the beginning of the spring semester of 1961, twenty-two students were assigned to an experimental class in remedial composition. This group, Group E, which was to be taught by the oral pattern practice method was also gathered largely on the basis of scores attained on the Cooperative English Test, Mechanics of Expression.

B. THE TESTING PROGRAM

1. *The Cooperative English Test*

The Cooperative English Test is a widely used objective test which consists of three major divisions: Reading Comprehension, Mechanics of Expression, and Effectiveness of Expression. Each is a forty minute examination. The test described in this study is the Mechanics of Expression, composed of Grammatical Usage, Punctuation and Capitalization, and Spelling. Part I, Grammatical Usage, consists of sixty sentences, each of which has four words underlined. The following directions are given in Form T which was used for the pre-test and post-test:

Read each sentence and decide whether there is an error in usage in any of the underlined parts of the sentence. If so, note the number printed under the wrong word or phrase, and put this number in the parenthesis at the right. If there is no usage error in the sentence, put a zero (0) in the parentheses. No sentence has more than one error, and some sentences do not have any errors. The sentences are to be judged on the basis of suitable usage for general written English.

Fifteen minutes are given for Part I. If a student has not finished a part before the time is up he must proceed to the next part. If he finishes a part, however, before the time is up, he may go on. He may at any time return to a preceding part if he has time. An alternate method by which a student can record his answers is the use of a machine-scored answer sheet. That method was used for the testing described here. The syntax and morphology items tested in Part I are subject-verb agreement, pronoun agreement, double negative, pronoun with gerund, comparisons, verb forms, adjective-adverb forms, pronoun case, subject redundancy, plurality ("three mile"), correlative forms, and parallel verb forms. When the errors of both groups of remedial students were isolated, the following types were found: subject-verb disagreement, pronoun disagreement, faulty comparisons, verb tense and sequence, adjective-adverb, plurality, faulty parallelism, run-on sentences, sentence fragments, preposition and sentence group modification, possessives, a-an errors. There is a close correlation, then, between the items tested in the Grammatical Usage part of the test and the items that were to be taught to both groups.

The first part of Section II tests the student's ability to punctuate at forty-five points in a number of sentences, not all of which are related. The directions for this section are:

In the passages below, at each place where there is a number below the line of text, decide what punctuation, if any, is needed there. At the right of that line, in the group numbered to correspond to the place in the text, locate the punctuation you consider correct for that place.

It is possible for the student to make run-on sentences, fragments, and errors in the possessive if he punctuates unwisely in this section. This section, along with the Grammatical Usage part makes the Mechanics of Expression test a valid instrument for determining the results of the experiment described here. The second section of Part II is entitled Capitalization. The total time given for both sections is fifteen minutes.

The directions in Part III, Spelling, are as follows: "In each of the items below, a word is spelled in two ways. Choose the correct spelling of the word, and put its number in the parentheses at the right...".

The Cooperative English Test is acknowledged by secondary schools, colleges and universities throughout the country to be a valid indication of the ability of students to communicate in English. The State University of New York, of which the State University College at Oswego is one unit, requires the test of all applicants to its forty-seven colleges and institutions. A number of schools throughout the country use this test alone, or with other tests and themes, to determine which students should be placed in a subfreshman composition course.[1] M. E. Gladfelter reports on,

a study concerned with the value of the cooperative English test as an instrument for the prediction of success at Temple University. It was hoped that the scores made on the three parts of this test might give information to substantiate that presented by the high school record and the [American Council] aptitude test. ... The intercorrelation between any of the measures ... indicates that as a single instrument for prediction one has no superiority over the other. It is interesting to note, nevertheless, that the *usage part* of the English test has as much value in itself as does the entire test. The correlation ... indicates that the test has as much predictive value for the freshman course in English composition as it has for general success in the freshman year.[2]

Because it tested what was being taught to both groups and because it has been accepted nationally as a good predictor of success, it was decided to use the Cooperative English Test as the major testing device for the experiment described in these pages.

Although syntax and morphology were the concern of this study, the use of all three parts of the Mechanics of Expression test, Grammatical Usage, Punctuation and Capitalization, and Spelling, was justifiable. The methods used to teach punctuation, capitalization, and spelling were the same for both the control and the experimental groups. Any difference in test scores, then, could be attributed only to the difference between the two methods of teaching syntax and morphology.

A low score on the Cooperative English Test was not the only criterion for determining whether a student would enter or remain in a remedial group. If a student was found to be writing on a subfreshman level in a regular section of freshman composition, he was transferred to a remedial section upon the consent of the instructor of that section, the present writer. On the other hand, if a student's writing was found to be on an acceptable level of achievement, he was dismissed from the course and put into a regular composition section.

The students in both groups studied, Group C, the control group, and Group E, the experimental group, were pre-tested with the Cooperative English Test, Form T, as a part of the battery of college entrance tests required by the State University of New York. Group C consisted of fourteen students taught in 1958 with a traditional textbook; Group E consisted of twenty-two students taught in 1961 with oral pattern practice materials designed by this writer after a close analysis of errors. The same form of the test was given to both groups upon the completion of their courses of study. It was partly on the basis of the mean difference between the two groups that the experimental method of teaching remedial English was deemed successful.

---

[1] "Has English Zero Seen Its Day? — A Symposium", *op. cit.*, pp. 72-95.
[2] M. E. Gladfelter, "Values of the Cooperative English Test in Prediction for Success in College", *School and Society*, 44 (September, 1936), p. 384.

2. *The Subjective Grading of Final Papers*

Another testing device that measured the success of the study was the subjective grading of final impromptu themes of three hundred words written by both groups. Each paper was read by three English instructors of the State University College to determine which of the students were ready to enter a regular section of freshman composition.

C. TEACHING AT THE POINT OF ERROR

It was the intention of the present writer to teach at the point of error for both groups, that is, to teach those items of syntax and morphology with which the students had most difficulty. The first problem was to determine whether or not an item was truly in error. In order to do this, the writer continually had to submit his analyses to his own judgment and that of modern linguistic findings. In addition, he had to recognize that other teachers in his department might work with his students after they had left the remedial English section, and so in some measure their attitudes toward language would have to prevail. All of these considerations were at one time or another brought to bear on the situation.

Finding the necessary items and subsequently teaching them were accomplished in a different way for each group. Group C, the control group, wrote fifteen themes of approximately three hundred words each, during the sixteen-week semester. The syntax and morphology items found to be in error were taught by using the *Macmillan Handbook of English*.[3] In this book one finds the traditional method of teaching by precept and written drill. Rules are explained to the student, who then writes out the exercises that appear at the close of each section.

The errors of Group E, the experimental group, were found by asking them to write two papers of approximately three hundred words during the first week of classes. This amounted to a total of ten thousand words. The frequencies of the types of errors found in these papers were similar to the frequencies found in twenty-five thousand words taken from Group C's papers, so it was determined that lessons could be devised by using Group E's errors as a basis. This is essentially what Pooley suggested be done in the first few weeks of school. The teacher should prepare a list of usage errors and analyze those that appear often in the students' writing.[4]

One may question whether a complete semester's course can be based on only ten thousand words written by students at the beginning of the semester. Stormzand and O'Shea state that their findings and those of Charters and Miller, and Roy Ivan Johnson reveal that:

---

[3]   John Kierzek, ed., *The Macmillan Handbook of English*, third edition (New York, The MacMillan Co., 1954).
[4]   Pooley, *op. cit.*, p. 185.

a relatively small amount of written material will give an accurate index of the relative importance of various errors for any particular group. ... In an elaborate investigation of the Kansas City Schools, Charters and Miller collected all the material in the form of written exercises handed in by the pupils during one month. After the study was completed, however, they stated that a single paper of 150 words from each pupil would have been sufficient to determine dependable conclusions.[5]

Stormzand and O'Shea do not mention another conclusion of some importance made by Charters and Miller. After they had collected data from all of the schools in Kansas City, they found that all the types of errors appeared in the first school studied.[6] It would seem, then, that ten thousand words provide a body of material large enough to determine the content of a composition course.

D. THE ORAL PATTERN PRACTICE METHOD

It has been stated that the general method by which Group E was taught was different from the studial method of reading and discussing precepts and then writing exercises at the close of a section, which was the method of Group C. With the oral pattern practice method of language learning the students were first told to observe a syntax or morphology phenomenon in a group of sentences. They then repeated the patterns after the instructor. This was an effort to make the students consciously aware of form and arrangement. For instance, when they were taught the differences between adjectives and adverbs, and their position in sentences, they were told to "observe the kinds of verbs and the forms of the modifiers found in the following sentences". Then they repeated after the teacher a number of sentences, such as:

Their work was easy.	They worked easily.
Mary was good.	She performed well.
He appeared slow.	He appeared quickly.
The slow man appeared.	The man appeared slowly.

The students were first encouraged to comment that there is a non-action verb with a subject that does not act (the distinction between this and the passive verb had to be discussed here), and an action verb with a subject that does act. They were then encouraged to comment that if a non-action verb such as *is* or *appeared* (looked to be) is followed by a modifier, the modifier will be in the adjective form; if an action verb such as *runs, performed,* or *appeared* (walked into view) is followed by a modifier, the modifier will be in the adverb or -ly form. The students learned inductively by generalizing only after they had repeated and observed the pattern.

The above discussion took only a small fraction of the total time allowed for

---

[5]   Stormzand and O'Shea, *op. cit.*, p. 174.
[6]   Charters and Miller, *op. cit.*, p. 16.

adjective-adverb forms. In order to make this particular pattern one of the habit patterns of the students, the oral practice pattern method was continued with the substitution and transformation exercises that follow:

Direction. In the following sentences *substitute* wherever it is possible and change the form of the modifier whenever it is necessary.

(Examples)

This work is easy.	THIS WORK IS EASY.
possible	THIS WORK IS POSSIBLE.
difficult	THIS WORK IS DIFFICULT.[7]

(Continue the exercise.)

1. impossible	7. serious
2. good	8. excellent
3. He eats (HE EATS WELL)	9. He writes
4. quickly	10. repeatedly
5. slowly	11. often
6. The speaker is	12. well

Direction. In the following sentences *transform* the sentence and the form of the modifier.

The quiet women waited.	THE WOMEN WAITED QUIETLY.
The slow man has run.	THE MAN HAS RUN SLOWLY.
One sleepy girl yawned.	ONE GIRL YAWNED SLEEPILY.

(Continue the exercise.)

1. The happy boy shouted.
2. Some careful men were looking.
3. An excited dog barked.
4. The expectant boy has been waiting.
5. His sincere young daughter talked.
6. The eager young man has been writing a letter.
7. An intelligent student answered his teacher's questions.
8. The anxious father looked for his son.
9. The glad audience listened to his speech.
10. One vigorous speaker has been lecturing.
11. The excellent teacher read the book.
12. The kind man will speak to the boys.

---

[7] The words in the lower-case letters were spoken by the teacher. Those in capital letters were spoken by the student, or students, whichever the teacher desired. The teacher spoke both parts in the examples and the students repeated after him. When they continued the exercise, the teacher spoke only his part and each student in turn, or all in chorus, spoke the predetermined form.

E. THE WRITING OF THE STUDENTS

1. *Writing Restricted Patterns*

The exercises were performed by the students chorally and individually. Each student had the advantage of either hearing or pronouncing each pattern enough times to make it an automatic response. At the end of the class hour students were given the mimeographed lesson or lessons they had just learned. They then read the material, *after* the attempt at habit forming, not before. For homework they wrote out the exercises they had recited orally in class. This had the effect of strengthening the newly learned habit pattern, and transferring it to their writing. This formed the bulk of the written work for Group E, although they were responsible for turning in several 350-word essays during the semester.

2. *Writing Themes*

Elements of good English other than syntax and morphology were taught to both groups, but were not the concern of the study described in these pages. Punctuation and capitalization were taught in great detail to both groups in the same manner, by using the *Macmillan Handbook of English*. In much less detail, but again in the same manner, both groups were taught the elements of good paragraphing, logic, diction, and spelling.

F. SUMMARY

In order to determine whether the oral pattern practice lessons would prove to be more effective for remedial students than traditional methods have been, Group C, a control group using traditional techniques, and Group E, an experimental group using the new lessons, had to be tested. It was decided that the objective testing device would be the American Council on Education's Cooperative English Test, Mechanics of Expression. Form T was used for the pre-test and the post-test. This is a test that has been widely used by colleges and universities to place students in remedial English sections, and it is acknowledged to give valid indication of a student's ability in English. Final impromptu essays by both groups also helped to grade progress in the course.

The lessons for Group E were devised by this writer after the students had written ten thousand words that were analyzed for non standard syntax and morphology constructions. Pattern practice exercises in repeating, substituting, and transforming taught standard structures at the points of error. The students later wrote out the exercises they had practiced orally in class in order to facilitate transferring the oral habits to writing. In addition, the students wrote several essays during the semester.

IV

THE ANALYSIS OF ERRORS AND THE METHODS OF CORRECTION

A. THE MATTER OF USAGE

In order to determine whether an item of syntax or morphology was in error, that is, non standard, this writer in great measure relied on the findings of linguistic studies.

1. *The Appeal to Linguistic Studies*

In the early 1930's, Sterling Leonard submitted to a number of judges, all well-educated people, a list of English constructions. Each judge decided whether or not each item was acceptable in English. On the basis of the returns, Leonard categorized each item and recorded his findings in a monograph published by the National Council of Teachers of English. If the item was approved for literary or good colloquial English by at least 75% of the judges, and disapproved by not more than 25%, it was con-considered an *established* usage. If it was approved by fewer than 75%, and disapproved by more than 25%, it was *disputable*. If it was disapproved by more than 75% and approved by fewer than 25%, it was an *illiterate* usage.[1]

If Leonard's findings reveal nothing else, they at least show the wide difference of opinion as to whether or not a single expression is established in its usage. But recording attitudes is not enough. Albert H. Marckwardt and Fred Walcott, feeling that the facts of usage deserved more careful attention than the attitudes toward the constructions, wrote in a later National Council monograph about Leonard's *disputable* items: "The appelative *disputable* is not appropriate in the description of a linguistic fact; it merely is an indication of the extreme variety of opinion."[2] An established usage, then, is one that appears in the language with some degree of frequency. There are cultural and economic levels of usage and an item might frequently appear on one level, but not on another.

The levels for which the teacher of English in college prepares his students are variously termed formal and informal, or literary and good colloquial (the latter terms are Leonard's). The college student preparing to take charge of community

---

[1] Sterling Andrus Leonard, *Current English Usage* (= *National Countil of Teachers of English Monographs*, 1) (Chicago, The Inland Press, 1932), p. 99.

[2] Albert H. Marckwardt and Fred G. Walcott, *Facts About Current English Usage* (New York, D. Appleton-Century Co., 1938), p. 33.

affairs is expected by the community to be able to write standard English on the formal level, and therefore should make this level a matter of habit.[3] The remedial course is intended to prepare students to write the language, not just to speak it. Because the written language is more formal than the spoken language, some of the findings of the linguists, who are concerned more with speech patterns than with written patterns, had to be disregarded for the purpose of this study.

2. *Other Considerations*

There were other considerations in determining whether or not a construction was to be classified as an error. Linguistic studies notwithstanding, this writer was forced in several instances to judge for himself whether or not an item was understandable or normal in the community which the student was preparing to enter. In addition, it had to be recognized that the writer's colleagues would later require his students to write in their composition and literature courses, and that their opinions, therefore, should prevail to some extent.

Many errors that were corrected during this study were *disputable*, according to Leonard's definition of the term. That is, there is a variety of opinions about them. This writer has found, however, that the greatest problem of a student needing remedial work is that so much of his syntax and grammar is disputable that the sheer weight of it makes the reader look on his writing as illiterate. The controversial items are discussed below.

B. THE STRUCTURES IN ERROR

1. *Verb Tense and Sequence*

The greatest number of errors found in the ten thousand words written by Group E was in the use of verb tenses and sequences. A great many of these were caused by the omission of affixes; most, in the omission of the *-ed*[4] morpheme in the past tense, and the *-ed/-en* morpheme in the past perfect tense. The *-s* morpheme indicating singularity was also omitted several times from the present tense. Most of the errors probably occurred because students were careless, as in the sentence: "Most of the team suffer injuries." But one or two might have been caused by a phonemic problem. In a sentence such as "That was when I decide to go", the close proximity of the verb base and the following phoneme /t/ (which is similar in sound to the necessary allomorph /id/) could account for the omission. Another phenomenon can account for this omission and that is the elimination of the final /-d/ in the base. The word "decided", then, is pronounced /disayid/ and might be spelled "decide".

---

[3] There is a specific designation, Standard English, Formal Level, which is used by Pooley, *op. cit.*, p. 21.
[4] The morphemic unit will be designated by italics rather than by the braces conventionally used in linguistic studies.

The pronunciation of the base might also contribute to omission in a sentence such as, "This hadn't dawn on me", where a hard-pronounced /n/ might in the student's mind take the place of /-d/, especially if /n/ is followed by vocalization. These are careless omissions. They are not the kinds of error that occur when a student lacks enough information to use the past perfect tense in place of the past tense, or when he abuses the historical present. They must be taught, however, to insure that the students will make the proper pronunciation and then the written verb tense automatic.

Another phonemic problem appeared in the verb tenses, but only once. That was the use of the word "of" in place of "have" in the sentence beginning "He may of been...". This no doubt occurred because "have" in this position and "of" can be homophones. This was not taught as a separate item, but included in other lessons.

The -ed and -s omissions were corrected in the experimental lessons designed by this writer to teach at the points of error. The class was first asked to observe the relationship between the verb ending and the time expressed. They then repeated the sentences:

John need ed	his warm coat	last night.
He arriv ed	safely	yesterday.
They walk ed	on the campus	last Friday.
It dawn ed	on him	as he drove home.
We hurri ed	to class	this morning.

The comments that followed the repetition noted that the -ed is affixed to the verb base with past time expressions. In the oral exercises that followed there were opportunities for the students to correct their errors caused by phonemic distortion as well as those caused by a misunderstanding of the relationship between past tense and time expressions (Note Lesson I in Appendix A).[5] At the conclusion of the class hour and after they had recited the exercises orally, the students were given the lesson sheets to prepare in writing for the next meeting. This gave them the opportunity to go over the material again and visually to note the position of the -ed morpheme. In like manner, the other verb forms found to be in error were taught. The only two errors not taught were an improper use of the infinitive, found in "I can ... to pass" and an intrusion of the affix -ing in "When the snow leaving early..." because they were thought to be anomalies.

Another usage found in students' writing that is not always accepted as standard was the structure "We will try and get it." There were only two such sentences, however, and they were not catalogued because this usage seems to be acceptable literary English, according to Marckwardt and Walcott.[6] Leonard also recognizes it as established.[7]

---

[5] The lessons in Appendix A are numbered in the order of their discussion in the present work, not in the order of their original presentation to the class.

[6] Marckwardt and Walcott, *op. cit.*, p. 34.

[7] Leonard, *op. cit.*, p. 124.

2. Run-On Sentences

Next in decreasing number of errors was the run-on sentence, in which two independent sentence structures were joined without proper punctuation. Although these sentences reflected errors in punctuation rather than in structure, they were included because this writer felt that the errors would be remedied if the student were made aware of syntax and morphology. Each of the second of the two joined structures was classified as either a "sequence" sentence, or a "non-sequence" sentence. The term "sequence" sentence was first suggested by Fries, who said in *The Structure of English*:

All the single free utterances or sentences, after the one at the beginning, constitute our 'sequence' sentences. In general, the forms of these 'sequence' sentences differ from those that stood first in the 'situation' utterance unit only in the fact that the 'sequence' sentences contain certain signals that tied them to the preceding utterances.[8]

Fries mentions several signals that tie sequence sentences to the utterances that precede them. They are: substitutes for Class I words; determiners and demonstratives; "else" and "other"; adverbs; and "so-called" conjunctions. The present writer found no evidence of the misuse of determiners or "else" and "other" in sequence sentences, but he did find evidence of other forms of sequence signals that were misused, one of them not mentioned by Fries. The largest share of run-on errors occurred when a pronoun, regular or demonstrative, was used as a substitute word in sequence sentences. Such a sentence was "... we come upon a strange mineral, it is black", in which "it" in the second sentence is a substitute for "mineral" in the first. The next largest block of errors occurred with the introduction in the sequence sentence of a form not mentioned by Fries. This was the repetition of a word found in the first utterance, as in "I heard a strange sound, I looked down".

A non-sequence sentence, this writer's term, is one that does not contain a signal that ties it to the immediately preceding utterance. Such a sentence found to be run-on was: "Then the big day came, I went to the music store." In the second utterance, "I went to the music store", there is no word tied to the first utterance, "Then the big day came."

It was possible to teach each of the sequence signals as a unit by forcing the student to make up a sequence of utterances using the signals he had been taught. He was asked, for instance, to put together a given sequence signal and a preceding sentence that would appear if the sentence were written. One such situation was: "It   He hit the ball squarely." The response would be something like: "He hit the ball squarely. It landed in the bleachers, just inside the foul line." The student knew before he responded that there were supposed to be two sentences, and he showed the division by a double-cross juncture and a prolonged pause between the two.

Working with sequence sentences prepared the students for the non-sequence structures, for the latter were taught in the same manner. The students were forced into forming sentence units after having been given determiners, sentence groups,

[8]   C. C. Fries, *The Structure of English* (New York, Harcourt, Brace and Co., 1952), p. 241.

nouns, pronouns, attention-getters, and question signals with which to begin. These were the introductory units of the sentence structures that had been improperly joined to preceding free utterances.

3. *Faulty Parallelism*

The greatest number of errors in parallelism were caused by a conflict between verb forms on either side of a parallel signal.[9] One such error was in the sentence, "I have seen many accidents happen and seen many close calls and I've been involved in the latter." There were errors not only in tense, but also in mood: This is what he likes best and is best suited for."

There were some mixtures of unlike parts of speech that also caused a lack of parallelism, as in "After some deep thought and looking back I knew what to do," in which a noun cluster and a verb form are unbalanced; and, "He told me of his troubles and how I must help", in which a preposition group and a sentence group are unbalanced.

The students first had to be made aware of the parallel signal and its function in the sentence. This was one of the clear opportunities to expand their vocabulary while developing their sentence sense. At times there seemed to be a direct relationship between a sparse vocabulary and poor structure, especially in sentence group modification, which will be discussed next. Fries has said this about the problem:

The most striking difference between [Standard English and Vulgar English] lay in the fact that Vulgar English seems essentially poverty stricken. It uses less of the resources of the language, and a few forms are used very frequently. *Get*, for example in its many senses appears in both the Standard English and the Vulgar English materials, but it is employed ten times as frequently in the Vulgar English letters as in those of Standard English. ... In vocabulary and in grammar the mark of the language of the uneducated is its poverty. ...[10]

All but three of the parallel signals found in Group E's papers were "and", so such items as "neither ... nor", "either ... or", and "not only ... but also" were supplied with blanks to be filled in orally with the balanced structures as a part of the sentence utterances.

4. *Preposition and Sentence Group Modification*

Misplaced modifying preposition and sentence groups accounted for several errors. Fries tells us that the fixed position of these groups, "has become that immediately following the word modified. In other words a prepositional phrase or a subordinate clause in general pattern modifies the word immediately preceding."[11] This is not always true, however, for an accepted position for the because/sentence group is at the

---

[9] Some of the parallel signals are "and", "for", "not only ... but also", "either ... or" and "neither ... nor".

[10] C. C. Fries, *American English Grammar* (New York, D. Appleton-Century Co., 1940), p. 288.

[11] *Ibid.*, p. 278.

beginning of the sentence, in which case it modifies the sentence utterance that follows it. In the papers were found such sentences as, "This rhythm was discovered by my mother in me at about the age of five", in which the preposition group "in me at about the age of five" modifies the noun "mother" rather than the verb "discovered".

These errors were corrected by making the students aware, first of all, that the preposition and sentence groups exist as modifying units, and secondly, that they exist in a certain position, according to their purpose. The oral exercises they then performed made the use of correct position habitual. Lesson II in Appendix A illustrates how this was done for the preposition groups.

Another of the problems that occurred with group modification was that faulty diction made them awkward. Such sentences as, "This is the part where everybody takes part in", and, "It is the part in which holds their attention" presented separate problems, but it was found they could be corrected in the same lesson. The first of the sentences presents a simple vocabulary problem. Disregarding for the moment the repetition of "part", the "where" should be replace by "which", and preceded by "in" if the instructor so desires. In the second sentence the "in" should be deleted.

In order to correct awkwardly joined groups, the students were first taught the difference between a who/sentence group and a because/sentence group. The who/sentence group is a subordinate clause introduced by a subordinator that is also the subject of the clause; the because/sentence group is introduced by a subordinator that precedes the subject of the clause. The vocabulary in the exercises that made the use of correct patterns habitual kept the students from making the sentence groups awkward. One of the vocabulary items that introduced the because/sentence groups in the lesson was "in which"; one of the items that introduced the who/sentence groups was "which". This vocabulary eliminated the errors in both sentences above. Although a sentence was not considered to be in error if it ended in a preposition, in the lessons on sentence groups the preposition preceded the subject and verb of the group because it can be classified as a part of the subordinator. When it appears in the subordinator position there is less possibility that the group will be joined awkwardly to the main clause. Lessons III and IV in Appendix A teach preposition and sentence group modification and correct errors in sentence fragments.

5. *Sentence Fragments*

It was assumed that although the errors listed in this section were errors in punctuation, they could be alleviated by directing the students' attention to syntax. Correcting sentence fragments was a natural adjunct to correcting sentence groups, because it was found that the majority of fragments were because/sentence groups that had been separated by a period and a capital letter from the words they modified. The because/sentence group, "If people would put the money they spend on beer into flying", for instance, was separated from the next sentence it modified, "They would probably live twice as long." Lesson IV in Appendix A, one of the lessons designed to correct fragments, shows how this error was corrected. Note, also, that there is some attention given to expanding the vocabulary items of the students. An increased vocabulary in this particular lesson helps the student avoid awkwardness caused by poor diction.

6. *Errors in the Plural*

Most of the errors in the plural form of nouns were caused by careless omission or intrusion of *-s*. Phonemic analysis fails to reveal a reason for the errors, however. In a sentence such as "There are two guard on the line", the student undoubtedly knew that the plural of "guard" is "guards". The context proves that; in the preceding sentence he had written about "two tackles" and "two ends". The sentence "One shoulders is within four inches of the mat" presents the same kind of error, carelessness. A phonemic analysis of this situation reveals nothing, unless one wants to say that the predominance of /-z/ in the words "is" and "inches" causes the intrusion.

Of a different nature were the inconsistencies in the plural such as in the following: "They would give you the shirts off their back." This revealed the students' lack of knowledge. A short lesson on this item was enough to correct the errors.

7. *Errors in the Possessive*

The omission of an apostrophe between a noun and the *-s* affix in the possessive is actually not an error in grammar, but in punctuation. It was treated in the same manner as a grammar error, however, by changing the possessive structure to "the ... of the ...' (note the apostrophe)" for the student. The placement of the apostrophe was no problem for him, because in this structure it always occurs in the same position, at the close of the statement. If in his mind the student was made immediately to change "every boys life..." to "the life of every boy'" and then back again, he placed the apostrophe in its proper position.

There were two examples of the omitted possessive in nouns appearing before gerunds, but they were included in neither the analysis of errors nor the lessons. Leonard labels this usage *established*,[12] and Marckwardt and Walcott claim it is accepted in literary English.[13] It was felt by this writer to be of little importance for remedial students when he compared it with the more flagrant errors reported here.

8. *Lack of Pronoun Agreement*

Pooley has said that "the rigid rules of the textbooks are not accurate in limiting the indefinite pronouns to singular use only. There are many occasions in English speech and writing in which the plural use is desirable for convenience, if not necessary."[14]

[12]   Leonard, *op. cit.*, p. 126.
[13]   Marckwardt and Walcott, *op. cit.*, p. 37.
[14]   Pooley, *op. cit.*, p. 91.

Pooley is not quite so liberal as one might conclude from this statement, however. He recognizes that it is only in the case of a resulting awkward structure, or in the case of an intervening plural word that the indefinite pronoun is plural. He lists among his errors to be eliminated in the high schools such structures as, "Everybody brought their friends" and, "Everyone helped themselves."[15] Regardless of the usage argument, it is to the advantage of the remedial student to learn that an item is either singular or plural. If the analysis becomes complex, as it would with inconsistencies or needless exceptions, he has difficulty making the correct response a matter of habit. That in itself should not be the final argument, of course, because the analysis should always be truthful, but in an area such as this in which there is some dispute, the simplest analysis should prevail. One of the indefinite pronouns, "none", was not treated, however, because there is little doubt that its number depends upon the sense of the preposition group that follows it, unless the situation is highly formal.

9. *Adjective–Adverb*

As might be expected, the greatest share of adjective-adverb errors occurred as a result of the omission of the *-ly* in adverbs. None of them was of the "slow-slowly" type that Leonard[16] and Marckwardt and Walcott[17] found acceptable in formal situations. They were of the kind they and Pooley found to be objectionable, such as "easy-easily".[18]

The distinction between "good" and "well" seemed to be a problem for several of the students, so it was taught and made a matter of habit in the pattern practices. Leonard discovered that opinion labeled the lack of distinction between the two *illiterate*,[19] and Marckwardt and Walcott called it *archaic*.[20]

A more controversial adjective-adverb problem than the above is the misplacing of words like "just" and "only" that should modify nouns or adjectives, but which modify verbs because of position. Such a sentence is, "He just does enough work." Again this writer relied on pedagogical efficiency to determine whether this item required re-structuring. Since confusion can result from this kind of construction, as in "He just walked fifteen miles", with at least two and perhaps three possible interpretations, it was decided to include the item in the lessons. It was felt here, too, that exceptions would prove disastrous to the students.

10. *Subject-Verb Disagreement*

Subject-verb disagreements presented a pedagogical problem for this study because there were so many error classifications. There was one item, however, that appeared

15   *Ibid.*, p. 218.
16   Leonard, *op. cit.*, p. 131.
17   Marckwardt and Walcott, *op. cit.*, p. 29.
18   Pooley, *op. cit.*, p. 220.
19   Leonard, *op. cit.*, p. 134.
20   Marckwardt and Walcott, *op. cit.*, p. 53.

often. It was the "There is" pattern with a plural subject. This has long been an accepted usage according to linguists. Pooley claims that because "the 'there is' combination is followed in the great majority of sentences by a singular subject it has become the standard way of introducing a subject, whether singular or plural, another example of victory of usage over logical grammar."[21] In his list of errors to be attacked, however, Pooley probably recognizes that logic must prevail in formal writing, and so he includes the following sentence: "There is several magazines on the table."[22] The correct structure was taught by forcing the students to substitute in the frame "There Vna-N" in which Vna represents a "non-action" or linking verb attached to the noun or its substitute, represented by N.

Two of the subject-verb disagreements listed here were singular collective nouns with plural verbs, as in the following sentence: "A football team consist of eleven men." In each of these sentences there was a plural phrase such as "eleven men" which suggested that the verb was meant to be plural, not singular. Therefore, the verb disagreed with its subject. If the student had meant the verb to be singular, the error would have been listed as a Verb Tense and Sequence error with an omitted -s affix.

Most of the remaining analyses of subject-verb disagreements showed that the remedial students had lost sight of the relationship between the subject and the verb because of intervening preposition and sentence groups. In the directions of the lesson that was taught at this point of error, the students were told to observe the subject-verb agreement. The examples that they repeated and the exercises they later recited had intervening preposition or sentence groups, some of them quite long. In the exercises the students had to repeat and form a sentence unit from a group of words such as the following: "The part of the chicken that I like best." The response could be "The part of the chicken that I like best is the leg." For the cue, "The parts of the chicken that I like best", the response might be, "The parts of the chicken that I like best are the legs and wings."

11. *Faulty Comparisons*

In the interest of efficiency it was also determined that the "I" form of the first person pronoun would prevail over the "me" form in the case of the comparison "I found myself with boys younger than me". This writer agrees with those who believe that this form is well established in the language, but because the "more/-er ... than" frame was not completed in several papers and so had to be taught, it was decided to keep all the pronouns following it in the same case. This structural simplification was less confusing than a more complex analysis might have been, and the nominative case of the first person pronoun is not incorrect in that position.

The comparison frame "as ... as" seems to be established, even in a negative sentence,

---

[21] *Ibid.*, p. 81.
[22] *Ibid.*, p. 219.

according to Leonard[23] and Marckwardt and Walcott,[24] so that frame was taught, rather than the "so ... as" frame. The intrusive "if not better" in "I could run as well, if not better, than the others" has not been accepted, however, and in the exercises it was attached to the conclusion of the utterances in which it appeared.

12. *A-An*

The omission of -n caused the smallest percentage of kinds of errors, but there were several of them. This error was not classified with adjectives because the article is thought of by this writer as a determiner, with special problems, largely phonemic, not associated with the adjectives. In student conferences it was found that people who omitted -n had a tendency to pronounce "a" /ey/. The /-y/ seems to bridge the two vowel sounds, then, in the place of /-n/. It was decided not to treat the omission of /-n/ as a separate lesson because it naturally would be a part of all the lessons. The mispronunciation of "a" was corrected in class and the distinction between "a" and "an" was in every lesson.

C. SUMMARY

The findings of descriptive linguists can in great measure determine whether a specific construction found in a student's writing is standard or nonstandard. The level of English usage for which the student is preparing must be recognized. Whether he needs remedial work or not, he is preparing to take charge of community affairs, and for that task he must be familiar with a formal level of writing.

The greatest number of errors in the ten thousand words written by remedial students were found to be in verb tense and sequence, and the omissions of affixes caused most of these errors. Run-on sentences were numerous, and it was found that there were both sequence and non-sequence sentences improperly joined to preceding sentences. Unbalanced verb forms caused the greatest number of errors in parallelism, but there were other errors caused by dissimilar parts of speech on either side of the parallel signal. Misplaced modifying preposition and sentence groups accounted for a good share of the total errors. Other nonstandard structures found were sentence fragments, errors in the plural forms of nouns, errors in the possessive, pronoun disagreement, adjective-adverb errors, subject-verb disagreement, faulty comparisons, and "a-an" confusion.

Each of the types of errors was given a descriptive analysis and pattern practice lessons were developed by this writer and used by him to rid the students of their specific errors.

[23] Leonard, *op. cit.*, p. 144.
[24] Marckwardt and Walcott, *op. cit.*, p. 27.

V

STATISTICAL FINDINGS

A. THE ANALYSIS OF ERRORS

1. *The Control Group*

Shortly before the spring semester of 1961, six 300-word themes from each of the fourteen students in Group C, the control group, were analyzed for types of syntax and morphology errors that the author assumed could most effectively be taught by an oral pattern practice method. There were twenty-five thousand words and 608 errors in syntax and morphology with which the author thought it feasible to experiment. This represented one error in grammar per forty-one words. There were errors in punctuation, capitalization, and other mechanics of writing that the author did not

TABLE 1

Types of Errors found in 25,000 Words Written by Group C

Type of Error	No. of Errors	%
Verb Tense and Sequence	133	21.89
Run-on Sentences	120	19.74
Faulty Parallelism	62	10.19
Preposition and Sentence Group Modification	57	9.37
Possessives	40	6.58
Lack of Pronoun Agreement	40	6.58
Subject-Verb Disagreement	37	6.09
Errors in the Plural	36	5.92
Faulty Comparisons	35	5.75
Sentence Fragments	25	4.11
Adjective-Adverb	17	2.79
A-An	6	.99
	608	100.00

compute for the experiment. Arranged in decreasing numerical order, the errors were in Verb-Tense and Sequence, 133 errors (21.89%); Run-On Sentences, 120 errors (19.74%); Faulty Parallelism, 62 errors (10.19%); Preposition and Sentence Group Modification, 57 errors (9.37%); Possessives, 40 errors (6.58%); Lack of Pronoun Agreement, 40 errors (6.58%); Subject-Verb Disagreement, 37 errors (6.09%); Plurals, 36 errors (5.92%); Faulty Comparisons, 35 errors (5.75%); Sentence Fragments, 25 errors (4.11%); Adjective-Adverb, 17 errors (2.79%); A-An, 6 errors (.99%). These errors, all listed in Table 1, had been made early in 1958.

2. *The Experimental Group*

During the first week of the spring semester of 1961, the twenty-two students in Group E, the experimental group, wrote two themes of approximately three hundred words each. A total of ten thousand words were analyzed to determine the number of errors of each type described above. There were 280 serious errors in sentence structure, or an average of one for every thirty-six words. Arranged in decreasing numerical order, they were found to be in Verb Tense and Sequence, 56 errors (20%); Run-On Sentences, 52 errors (18.49%); Faulty Parallelism, 30 errors (10.71%); Preposition and Sentence Group Modification, 27 errors (9.64%); Plurals, 20 errors (7.14%); Possessives, 19 errors (6.78%); Lack of Pronoun Agreement, 19 errors (6.78%); Adjective-Adverb, 15 errors (5.36%); Subject-Verb Disagreement, 14 errors (5.00%);

TABLE 2

Types of Errors found in 10,000 Words Written by Group E

Type of Error	No. of Errors	%
Verb Tense and Sequence	56	20.00
Run-on Sentences	52	18.59
Faulty Parallelism	30	10.71
Preposition and Sentence Group Modification	27	9.64
Errors in the Plural	20	7.14
Possessives	19	6.78
Lack of Pronoun Agreement	19	6.78
Adjective-Adverb	15	5.36
Subject-Verb Disagreement	14	5.00
Faulty Comparisons	13	4.64
Sentence Fragments	10	3.57
A-An	5	1.79
	280	100.00

Faulty Comparisons, 13 errors (4.64%); Sentence Fragments, 10 errors (3.57%); A-An, 5 errors (1.79%). These errors are listed in Table 2.

Because both of the groups listed the first four types in the same order and because the percentages of error were similar for all types in both groups, it was assumed that the errors found in the ten thousand words of Group E represented those that would normally appear in the writing of New York State college students in need of remedial English composition. A closer analysis of the types in Group E was then undertaken with the results as shown in Table 3 in Appendix B.

B. FINDINGS OF THE EXPERIMENT

1. *The Pre-Test Scores of the Control Group*

In the spring of 1958, on the basis of scores made on the Cooperative English Test, Mechanics of Expression, Form T, thirteen students were chosen to enter Group C to take remedial freshman composition. Another student volunteered to enter the course and permission was granted by the instructor, who was familiar with his written work. This brought the total to fourteen in Group C. The test scores ranged from thirty to fifty-two. The mean standard score was 40.36, which placed them, according to norms for public secondary schools of the East, Middle West, and West, between the eighth and ninth grades, and below the national norm of 48.10 for freshmen entering junior colleges and teachers colleges.[1]

2. *The Pre-Test Scores of the Experimental Group*

In the spring of 1961, twenty-two students entered Group E for remedial freshman composition. These students were chosen on the basis of scores attained on the Cooperative English Test, Mechanics of Expression, Form T, and on the recommendations of teachers of freshman composition at the end of the first week of the semester. The test scores ranged from thirty to fifty-six. The mean standard score of this group was 44.00, which placed them in the ninth grade, and below the national norm of 48.10. This was 3.64 points higher than the mean of Group C.

In order to be certain that the difference between these two groups was statistically insignificant, a t-test was computed.[2] The t-test result was 1.87, or less than the possible margin of 2.042. The two groups, therefore, were determined to be equal at the onset of the experiment.

---

[1]   The ranks for junior colleges and teachers colleges will be referred to because at the time of the experiment the State University College at Oswego was a teachers college. It has since become a dual-purpose liberal arts-teacher training institution.

[2]   The t-ratio is a statistical estimate to determine how often a found difference between means would appear purely on the basis of chance. If the result shows that the chance occurrence of the obtained difference or more would be less than 5 in 100, then it is conventionally interpreted to mean that there is a significant difference.

3. *The Post-Test Scores of the Control Group*

On the re-test administered at the conclusion of the sixteen weeks of classes, the following scores were attained. The range of scores for Group C was thirty-two to fifty-three, with a mean of 44.79. This represented a change of +4.43. The score placed this group midway between the ninth and tenth grades, and still below the national norm of 48.10 for entering freshmen. A t-test determined that the difference between the pre-test and post-test mean scores of this group was statistically significant. The t-test result was 2.86, or beyond the margin of 2.042 (P < .005).[3]

4. *The Post-Test Scores of the Experimental Group*

On the re-test, the range of scores for Group E was thirty-one to sixty. The mean was 50.14, which represented a change of +6.14. This placed the group in the eleventh grade and 2.04 points above the national norm for freshmen entering junior colleges and teachers colleges. A t-test determined that the difference between the pre-test and post-test mean scores of this group was also statistically significant. The t-test result was 5.90, well beyond the margin of 2.042 (P < .0005).

5. *The Difference between the Two Groups*

In order to determine whether or not the experimental Group E learned significantly more than the control Group C, it was necessary to show that there was a significant difference between the post-test scores of the two groups and that the difference was in favor of Group E. As already related, there was no significant difference between their pre-test scores.

A t-test was computed to determine the difference in post-test scores with a result of 3.47, well above the margin of 2.042. This showed a significant difference between the two groups, with the difference in favor of Group E with its greater mean score. The results of this testing are found in Table 4.

TABLE 4

Mean Differences between Pre- and Post-Test Means for Each Group

Group	Pre-Test Mean	Post-Test Mean	Mean Difference	t-values	P
Group C	40.36	44.79	4.43	2.86	.005
Group E	44.00	50.14	6.14	5.98	.0005

[3] P < .005 means that the probability (P) that different results of the magnitude found or greater will occur in retesting under the same conditions is 5 in 1000. A difference of this size is rare. It is therefore interpreted as a significant difference.

6. *The Relative Changes in Rank Order*

It was decided not only to compile the mean differences of Groups C and E, but also to observe rank orders and compute correlation factors of both groups. The correlation factor between the pre- and post-tests in the control group had a Rho factor of. 65 (Rho = .65). This means that the degree of agreement in individual rank orders between the pre- and post-tests of Group C was fairly high.[4] A t-test estimated the change as significantly greater than 0. The correlation factor between the pre- and post-tests of Group E was found to be .2, which means that many students shifted their rank in the group between the pre- and post-tests. A t-test established this, also, to be a significant difference.

The degree of relative change in rank order of Group E suggests that the experimental variable was effective in producing individual shifting. This is paralleled by the fact that the experimental group had a greater raw score gain.

7. *The Results of the Subjective Test*

The subjective test described in Chapter III bears out the objective data found above. Three instructors from the English Department of the State University College at Oswego graded final three hundred-word compositions of both groups. On the basis of these compositions, eight of the fourteen in Group C were admitted to a regular freshman composition course (57.1 %). All of the twenty-two students in Group E were admitted to freshman composition (100 %).

C. SUMMARY

The types of errors in ten thousand words of Group E's writing showed a similarity to the types found in twenty-five thousand words from Group C, so it was decided that a closer analysis of Group E's errors would prove worthwhile upon which to base a course in remedial English. This suggests, also, that the description of errors found in this study would prove useful to anyone teaching a group of students similar to the one taught here. This was a group of freshman students in a New York State college from nearly all areas of the state.

There were 280 syntax and grammar errors in the ten thousand words, with the errors in subject-verb disagreement, run-on sentences, lack of parallelism, and misplaced and dangling modifiers causing nearly seventy percent of all the errors.

---

[4] The correlation factor (Rho) indicates how much two sets of scores agree in their rank order of paired scores. The rank order of each student in the class is determined at the beginning of the instruction and at the conclusion of it. If the rank order of each student is the same before and after instruction there will be a Rho factor of 1.00 (Rho = 1.00). The greater the change in rank order, the smaller is the correlation. A low correlation, then, indicates considerable shift in rank orders.

The testing revealed that the oral pattern practice method, at least as found in the lessons described in this study, is more effective than the more traditional studial approach. The t-value of Group C was 2.86 and the t-value of Group E was 5.98. The subjective test revealed that eight of the fourteen students in Group C were to be admitted to a regular freshman composition class; all twenty-two of the students in Group E were to be admitted to freshman composition. It could not be assumed that the greater improvement in the scores of Group E was caused by a greater effort on the part of the teacher. The oral pattern practice method of teaching Group E was decided upon, and the lessons devised, only after the teacher had already taught Group C to the best of his ability.

VI

RECOMMENDATIONS

A. UTILIZING THE ORAL PATTERN

In the light of the testing results described in Chapter V, it is recommended that oral pattern practice lessons based on a description of students' errors in syntax and morphology form the course of instruction for students in need of remedial English composition.

B. UTILIZING THE ERRORS DESCRIBED IN TABLE 3

It is felt by this writer that the errors described in Table 3 in Appendix B can form the basis for remedial freshman courses in New York State and in similar dialect areas. The errors were found in a body of ten thousand words written by remedial students and were similar in frequency to those found in twenty-five thousand words written earlier by another group of students in need of corrective study.

It is further recommended that an instructor from a dialect area different from New York State develop his own oral pattern practice lessons by basing them on a close analysis of errors found in several three hundred-word student essays written at the beginning of the semester.

C. MAKING GRAMMATICAL GENERALIZATIONS

A student should make his own grammatical generalizations if they are to be made at all, and they should be the result of inductive reasoning. He can be told which structure to observe in a series of sentences, and upon repeating the sentences after the teacher he should generalize about the structure.

D. ADDITIONAL NEEDS

There are ways in which a remedial course can be made more effective than the experimental Group E's was. The method described here is important enough, and the problems of the students are great enough so that more time should be devoted to the work. Certainly a great deal more work could be handled in a laboratory. Taped lessons could be designed that would make use of the oral practice pattern method and other modern language learning procedures. More class hours are needed, also. It is almost unnecessary to say that too little can be done for a remedial student in a college class that meets only three hours a week for sixteen weeks. This might suggest that the remedial course should be taught in secondary schools and for a full school year. Then the teacher and the students could devote two hundred hours to it instead of forty-eight.

Although there was a statistically significant difference between the pre- and post-test scores of Group E, it was felt that the lessons would have been more than doubly effective had there been even twice the number of hours devoted to them. Each lesson was taught during only one class hour, and then not during every one of the class hours available because time had to be spent on non-grammatical errors. If the students had had the opportunity to review each of the lessons with additional exercises, at the end of the course, their ability to recall the work would theoretically have been much greater.

E. THE STUDENTS' ABILITY TO DO THE WORK

The students seem able to take large doses of oral drill. In the English Language Institute at the University of Michigan, students practice patterns orally three hours a day, five days a week, for eight weeks. This is done in their grammar classes and in the laboratory with taped lessons. There are two additional hours of class each day, but they are not devoted to oral pattern practice. Although the experimental students in Group E met in the late afternoon after nearly all of them had just completed a three-hour laboratory class, there seemed to be neither boredom nor diminishing returns as a result of the lessons. There certainly was no boredom, and both the teacher and the students felt that the returns were sustained. Three weeks before the close of the semester, all of the students asked that the class meet five days a week, rather than three days a week. Later, every student asked that the class meet during final examination week, a time traditionally closed to the meeting of classes. At the close of the semester, each student petitioned the Dean of the College that he be given a second semester of the same course under the same conditions.

There are non-grammatical problems that loom large in the writing of remedial composition students. Vocabulary, spelling, capitalization, and punctuation are problems usually separate from syntax and morphology, but just as difficult to teach and they should get more treatment than was possible in the course described here. Vocabulary is the least of these problems, however, because unfamiliar words can be included in familiar contexts within the frames taught to the students. That was modestly attempted in this study.

APPENDIX A

LESSON I: THE PAST TENSE OF THE VERB

Observe the relationship between the verb ending and the time expressed.

S V -ed			Time expression
John need	ed	his warm coat	last night.
He arriv	ed	safely	yesterday.
They walk	ed	on the campus	last Friday.
It dawn	ed	on him	as he drove home.
We hurri	ed	to class	this morning.

Comment:

1. The -ed form of the verb (V-ed) is used with past time expressions.

Exercise: Substitute wherever necessary, and change all the verbs into the past tense (V-ed).

They arranged the meeting yesterday.	THEY ARRANGED THE MEETING YESTERDAY.
we	WE ARRANGED THE MEETING YESTERDAY.
started	WE STARTED THE MEETING YESTERDAY.

(Continue the exercise.)

1. after class
2. the game
3. an hour ago
4. the fire
5. the car
6. he paints
7. three weeks ago
8. our picture
9. deliver
10. look for

11. a week ago Tuesday
12. arrive safely
13. my aunt
14. yesterday
15. recognize a friend
16. on the campus
17. Joe recognized a friend
18. meet Sally
19. decide to walk
20. study

Exercise: Transform the following, and change all the verbs into the past tense (V-ed).
         Repeat the last statement in each of the following examples.

Yesterday   I wait for the bus   I WAITED FOR THE BUS YESTERDAY.
last Sunday   They hurry to church   THEY HURRIED TO CHURCH LAST SUNDAY.
after that   I go to school   I WENT TO SCHOOL AFTER THAT.

(Continue the exercise.)
 1. last night   I see the man
 2. Wednesday   They arrange a conference
 3. last week   She irons her family's clothes
 4. then   They ask for a raise
 5. after breakfast   We paint
 6. when we moved   We pack carefully
 7. several Fridays ago   We start
 8. after school   We move
 9. last month   They study for their tests
10. yesterday afternoon   Jim works hard
11. a week later   He reports the accident
12. before dinner last night   I work in the garden
13. once after that   I play tennis
14. three years ago   They live downtown
15. last Tuesday   We consult a lawyer
16. afterward   I deliver the message
17. Monday   They order their groceries
18. during last night's accident   We need distress signals
19. then   He helps his father
20. later   Joe walks in the park

LESSON II: THE PREPOSITION GROUP AS A MODIFIER

Observe the function and the position of the preposition group (P-grp).

	Modified	Modifier	
	The bracelet	under the archway	was found by her friend.
The bracelet was found by	her friend	under the archway.	
The bracelet	was found	under the archway	by her friend.
		Under the archway	the bracelet
	was found	by her friend.	

Comments:

1. The preposition group (P-grp) "under the archway" modifies, and usually follows the modified word.
2. The P-grp can be placed before the subject of the verb it modifies, as it does in the last sentence.
3. The phrase "by her friend" is also a P-grp that modifies "was found" in the last sentence.

Exercise[1]: Below are two sentences. Form a new sentence by putting the P-grp suggested in the second sentence into the first one.

She sat and watched her son. She was in the audience.
SHE SAT IN THE AUDIENCE AND WATCHED HER SON.
He was in the audience.
SHE SAT AND WATCHED HER SON IN THE AUDIENCE.
The cat jumped when the dog appeared. It went up a tree.
THE CAT JUMPED UP A TREE WHEN THE DOG APPEARED.
It had been up the tree.
THE CAT UP THE TREE JUMPED WHEN THE DOG APPEARED.

(Continue the exercise.)

 1. She went to call the child. The child was behind the house.
 2. She was behind the house.
 3. His watch fell into the pond. The pond was near the house.
 4. It fell in near the house.
 5. He called his family. They were at the lake.
 6. He was at the lake.
 7. They left the party. The party took place before the dance.
 8. They left before the dance.
 9. All the boys saw the cat. It was in the car.
10. They were in the car.
11. Some men saw the green, unripe apple. It was on the ground.
12. They were on the ground.
13. They looked at the boat. It was by the river.
14. They were by the river.
15. The sheriff looked for the girl. She was with the dog.
16. He was with the dog.
17. We drove while it snowed. We were in the car.
18. It was a convertible and the top was down.
19. He walked as the party progressed. He went out the door.
20. They went out the door.

[1] The exercise appears here as it was when this lesson was taught to Group E. It has since been revised. The revision immediately follows this exercise.

REVISED EXERCISE: Below are two sentences. Form a new sentence by putting the
P-grp suggested in the second sentence into the first one.

She sat and watched her son. She was in the audience.
SHE SAT IN THE AUDIENCE AND WATCHED HER SON.
He was in the audience.
SHE SAT AND WATCHED HER SON IN THE AUDIENCE.
The cat jumped when the dog appeared. It went up the tree.
THE CAT JUMPED UP THE TREE WHEN THE DOG APPEARED.
The cat was up the tree.
THE CAT UP THE TREE JUMPED WHEN THE DOG APPEARED.

(Continue the exercise.)
1. She went to call the child. The child was behind the house.
2. She went behind the house.
3. His watch fell into the pond. The pond was near the house.
4. It fell in near the house.
5. He called his family. They were at the lake.
6. He was at the lake.
7. All the boys saw the cat. It was in the car.
8. They were in the car.
9. Some men saw the green, unripe apple. It was on the ground.
10. They were on the ground.
11. They looked at the boat. It was by the river.
12. They were by the river.
13. The sheriff looked for the girl. She was with the dog.
14. He was with the dog.
15. He drove while it snowed. We were in the car.
16. It was a convertible and the top was down.
17. He looked as the men ran. He looked out the door.
18. They went out the door.

LESSON III: THE SENTENCE GROUP (S-grp) AS A NOUN MODIFIER

Observe the position and function of the sentence group (who/S-grp).

	Sub	Who/S-grp
A person	WHO	has no education is not usually well paid.
Fido is a cat	THAT	likes milk.
There is a chair	WHICH	looks comfortable.
He gave me twenty cents	WHICH	was better than nothing.

Comments:

1. "Who has no education" is called a who/sentence group (who/S-grp) because it has a subject, "who", and a verb, "has".
2. The S-grp here modifies, or is subordinate to, a noun, "Person", and immediately follows it.
3. The S-grp occurs within a sentence, or at the end of one.
4. Who, etc., are called "Who-Subordinators".
5. WHO refers to a person, WHICH to a thing, and THAT to either a person or a thing.
6. An S-grp cannot stand alone.

Exercise: Listen to the following noun and S-grp modifier. Student A will produce a sentence with the S-grp within a sentence; Student B will produce one with the S-grp at the end of one.

The unfortunate student who has not yet found the answer

Student A: THE UNFORTUNATE STUDENT WHO HAS NOT YET FOUND THE ANSWER WILL BE UP LATE TONIGHT.

Student B: JIM IS THE UNFORTUNATE STUDENT WHO HAS NOT YET FOUND THE ANSWER.

The young man that saw John

Student C: THE YOUNG MAN THAT SAW JOHN HAS MANY FRIENDS.

Student D: SHE SPOKE WITH THE YOUNG MAN THAT SAW JOHN.

(Continue the exercise.)

 1. Some tables which are unsteady
 2. The author who lectured
 3. A tree that had lost its leaves
 4. The river which goes by the house
 5. Some women who stayed up late
 6. An elderly lady that felt faint
 7. The gate which banged
 8. All people who make long speeches
 9. A few cats that were on the fence
10. Those girls who will talk steadily

LESSON IV: THE BECAUSE/SENTENCE GROUP (SENTENCE FRAGMENTS)

Observe the position and function of the S-grp.

	Sub	Because/S-grp
He spoke fluently	BECAUSE	he was a native.
George is the one	WHOM	she likes.
There is a store	INTO WHICH	I frequently go.
I saw a friend	WHOM	I trust

Comments:

1. Unlike the "Who-Subordinator", the "Because-Subordinator" is not the subject of the verb.
2. "Whom she likes" is called a sentence group (S-grp) because it has a subject, *she*, and a verb, *likes*.
3. The S-grp here modifies, or is subordinate to, a noun, "one", or a verb, "spoke", and follows the modified word.
4. The "Because-Subordinator" connects two sentence patterns.
5. An S-grp cannot stand alone.

Exercise: Listen to the following subordinators and sentence pattern.
          Produce an S-grp connected to the sentence pattern.
which   Here is the tree
HERE IS THE TREE WHICH GEORGE CLIMBED.
because   He won the race
HE WON THE RACE BECAUSE HE HAD TRAINED WELL.

(Continue the exercise.)

1.	whose	Jack is the boy
2.	that	I know
3.	because	She couldn't hear
4.	when	She smiles
5.	if	Jane will do the work
6.	whom	There is only one there
7.	while	He read a magazine
8.	since	I have not seen him
9.	because	Jane knew her lines
10.	before	Jim went to Chicago
11.	since	It has been three years
12.	until	She would not drive a car
13.	whether or not	I must go
14.	while	The child played with his toys
15.	unless	I won't go downtown
16.	because	He passed his Latin examination
17.	although	He failed his mathematics examination
18.	in which	This is the house
19.	after	We cleaned the house
20.	in whom	My mother is a person

APPENDIX B

TABLE 3

An Analysis of 280 *Syntax and Morphology Errors Found in* 10,000 *Words Written by Remedial Composition Students*

VERB TENSE AND SEQUENCE

Error	No. Errors		%
Omission of *-ed* affix			
/-d/ allomorph omitted in the past tense (Most of the team *suffer* injuries.)[a]	4		
/-id/ in past (That was when I *decide* to go.)	2		
		6	2.14
Omission of *-ed*/-*en* affix			
/-d/ in past perfect (This hadn't *dawn* on me.)	2		
/-d/ in present perfect (I might have *figure* out …)	2		
/-d/ in passive present (… that must be *learn*.)	2		
		6	2.14
Omission of -s affix			
/-z/ in present singular (… this school *hold* for me.)		3	1.07
Errors in the past perfect tense			
Improper use of past (I called the store where I *bought* a pump.)		9	3.21
Errors in the present perfect tense			
Past perfect (He is the one who *had compiled* the most points.)	2		
Past + "since" (I *played* … each summer, since my junior year.)	2		
Auxiliary + "of" + perfect (He may *of* been …)	2		
Passive past + present perfect time expression (He foresaw the advances that *were made* in the last few years.)	2		
		8	2.86

TABLE 3 (*Continued*)

Error	No. Errors			%
Errors in the past tense				
Abused historical (After a few breaks I *get* into college.)	5			
Present perfect (I have worked since *I've been* twelve.)	1			
		6		2.14
Vna in place of Va[b] (A touchdown *is* [occurs] when the team carrying the ball ...)		5		1.79
Preposition + V-ing[c] in place of an infinitive (I must help *in replacing* a broken part.)		4		1.43
Omission of the verb (It just that ...)		4		1.43
Omission of the apostrophe in contracted forms (Youre)		3		1.07
Improper use of infinitive (I can ... *to pass*)		1		.36
Intrusion of the verb affix *-ing* (when the show *leaving* early ...)		1		.36
			56	20

[a]   The examples are taken from the papers of the remedial composition students.
[b]   "Vna" represents a non-action or intransitive verb. "Va" represents an action or transitive verb.
[c]   "V-ing" represents the form of the verb in which the morpheme *-ing* is affixed to the base.

RUN-ON SENTENCES

Joining Sequence Sentences Without Proper Punctuation

Error	No. Errors			%
When a pronoun is used as a substitute word				
"it" (... we come upon a strange *mineral, it* is black.)	6			
"they" (I will never forget the first *days* of practice *they* were murder.)	3			
"that" (I would go into *service that's* an easy life.)	3			
"this" (Another function is *stealing* the ball, *this* requires ...)	1			
"I" (This caused *me* to wonder what had gone wrong, hadn't *I* ...)	1			
		14		5.00
Use of a P-grp[d] as a substitute word (*Millions* of spectators watch *from eight to eighty* enjoy this sport.)		1		.36
When a word from the first sentence structure is repeated				
"I ... I" (I heard a strange sound, *I* looked down.)	8			
"we ... we" (I can't say we had too much work, *we* read novels.)	1			

TABLE 3 (*Continued*)

Error	No. Errors				%	
"why ... why" (Why should I tell them, *why* don't I ...)	1					
		10			3.57	
Use of an adverb (That setled it for awhile *then* I ...)		3			1.07	
		28			10.00	

d   "P-grp" represents a preposition group.

Joining Non-Sequence Sentences Without Proper Punctuation

Error	No. Errors		%	
"the" (But that's not so, *the* days of Honest Abe are gone forever.)	5		1.79	
Introductory S-grp[e] (I wasn't sure of what to expect *as I attended high school*, I heard tales about college.)	5		1.79	
Pronoun (Then the big day came, *I* went to the music store.)	4		1.43	
Interjection (Then came the first day *boy* was I nervous.)	4		1.43	
Noun (The bigger the person the more control a person can have *strength* is also important.)	2		.71	
"it" (If he likes it O.K. *it* doesn't make much difference.)	1		.36	
"this" (The idea gave me a feeling ..., *this* is the way I would describe it ...)	1		.36	
Question signal (That's not much of a life *who* wants to be a private.)	1		.36	
Repeating conjunction (College is the answer *but* how to get into college *but* give it a try.)	1		.36	
		24		8.59
		52		18.59

e   "S-grp" represents a sentence group or dependent clause.

FAULTY PARALLELISM

Error	No. Errors				%	
Verb + verb (tense)						
V-ing + V[f] (After *living* there and *walk* over the land ...)	3					
AuxV-en + V-en[g] (I *have seen* many accidents happen and *seen* many ...)	2					
to-V + V-ing (... ability *to discuss* a variety of subjects and *being* able ...)	2					

TABLE 3 (*Continued*)

Error	No. Errors		%	
Aux V-ing + V (What a bookworm *is lacking* in social standing, a playboy *lacks* in education.)	2			
		9		3.21
Active V + passive V (This is what he *likes* best and *is best suited* for.)		2		.71
Verb + verb cluster (This teacher *used* and *worked a lot in the social aspects of our high school.*)		2		.71
Verb + omitted verb (Every day it was *put* on the sneakers and on the court.)		2		.71
Verb + noun				
Noun cluster + V-ing (After *some deep thought* and *looking* back ...)	3			
Verb cluster + noun cluster (... from *trying to score* to *that of trying to stop the scoring.*)	2			
V-ed[h] + noun (The way she *talked*, and her *expressions* were magnificent.)	2			
		7		2.50
Noun + noun cluster (... the reading of *poems* and *similar types of reading.*)		2		.71
Preposition groups				
P-grp + noun (... man is capable *of these kinds of injustices* and *justice* to himself.)	2			
P-grp + S-grp (He told me *of his troubles* and *how I must help.*)	1			
		3		1.07
Modifier-noun + modifier (The most popular science fiction is not the "*way out type*" but the "*it could happen to you*".		2		.71
Who/S-grp[i] + who/S-grp with omitted subordinator (... the part *that is a shame* but *must be faced*)		1		.36
		30		10.71

[f] "V" represents a verb. The infinitive is represented by "to-V".

[g] "Aux" represents an auxiliary verb. "V-en" represents the perfect tenses of the verb.

[h] "V-ed" represents the past tense of the verb.

[i] "Who/S-grp" represents a sentence group in which the subordinator is also the subject of the group. In this particular sentence, "that" is a who/subordinator. The who /subordinator, "which", is missing after the word "but".

TABLE 3 (*Continued*)

PREPOSITION AND SENTENCE GROUP MODIFICATION

Error	Correct Form	No. Errors			%
Misplaced modifiers					
Noun + P-grp (This rhythm was discovered by my *Mother in me* ...)	Verb + P-grp	4			
Wrong verb + who/S-grp (Your team mate will rush to your aid if the man *has* the ball *in order to prevent the score*.)	Modify correct verb.	3			
Noun + "there" adverb (As an entering *freshman, last fall,* I went out for soccer.)	Verb + "there" adv.	2			
"Then" + "there" adverb (My hopes of having a better season *next fall on the soccer field* have kept ...)	"there + then"	2			
			11		3.93
Improper forms of the modifier					
"The reason is ..." (I found myself with younger boys. *The reason* for this *is* ...)	"because"	4			
Improper diction (This is the part *where* everybody takes part *in*.)	"in which"	2			
Because/S-grp[1] (It is the part *in which* holds their attention.)	Who/Sub-ordi-nator ("which")	2			
P-grp (It provides people with pleasure and jobs *for many*.)	Adv	2			
			10		3.57
Dangling modifiers					
V-ing, incorrect subject (*When camping, life* seems [simple].)		5			
Infinitive, incorrect subject (*To carry* him through the air *he* has created the airplane.)		1			
			6		2.14
				27	9.64

[1] "Because/S-grp" represents a sentence group in which the subordinator is also the subject of the group. "In which" is a because/subordinator.

TABLE 3 (*Continued*)

SENTENCE FRAGMENTS[k]

Error	No. Errors		%	
Because/S-grp (*If* people would put the money they spend on beer into flying.)	5		1.79	
Noun + who/S-grp (The *part that* is a shame to think about.)	2		.71	
Noun + V-ing (Each member *doing* his share.)	2		.71	
V-en (More commonly *known* as giving alibis.)	1		.36	
		10		3.57

[k] Although sentence fragments are not next in descending numerical order, they are tabled here because there is a close relationship between them and S-grp modification.

ERRORS IN THE PLURAL

Error	No. Errors			%		
Omission of -*s*						
Carelessness (There are *two guard* on the line.)	10					
Conflict between "they/their" and noun (They would give you the *shirts* off their *back*.)	2					
		12		4.29		
Intrusive -s						
Word thought of as collective (Even the littlest *things*, which this certainly was, can cause depression.)	3					
Carelessness (One *shoulders* is within four inches of the mat.)	2					
Mod s + Npl[l] (At the *next* full *practices* we went over the plays.)	1					
		6		2.14		
Diction (We took a trip to see *a* Broadway play, "Much Ado About Nothing", and "My Fair Lady".)	2			.71		
			20			7.14

[l] "Mod" represents a modifier. "s" means that the modifier is singular. "N" represents a noun, and "pl" means that it is plural.

ERRORS IN THE POSSESSIVE

Error	No. Errors			%	
Omission of apostrophe					
In possessive noun before a noun (In every boys life ...)	15				

TABLE 3 (*Continued*)

Error	No. Errors			%	
In possessive noun before an omitted noun (He stays at my home or at my *roommates*.)	2				
		17		6.05	
Apostrophe following -*s* (... a *referees'* position on the mat.)		1		.36	
Apostrophe in a plural (... two or three *day's*.)		1		.36	
			19		6.78

LACK OF PRONOUN AGREEMENT

Error	No. Errors		%	
Shift to indefinite "you/they" not in same sentence (In high school there are twelve weight classes. *They* are allowed to gain two pounds.)	9		3.21	
Singular pronoun + "they/their" (*No one* will ever understand unless *they* go skiing.)	4		1.43	
Singular noun + "they/their" (First came the sea *life*; *they* became ...)	2		.71	
Collective noun + Vs + "they" (The team *has* a chance to kick or *they* may elect to run.)	2		.71	
Plural pronoun + "he" (*All* feel a part of it, even if *he* is only a fan.)	1		.36	
Shift to indefinite "you/they" in same sentence. (*We* would get nervous and feel a hollow feeling in *your* stomach.)	1		.36	
		19		6.78

ADJECTIVE — ADVERB

Error	No. Errors		%	
Verb + Adj. (It didn't work out that *easy*.)	6		2.15	
"Good-Well" (That worked out pretty *good*.)	3		1.07	
Adj. modifier + Adv. (In no other activity is the family brought so *close* together.)	2		.71	
Adv. + Verb instead of Adj. + Adj. (He *just* does enough work.)	2		.71	
"Most-Almost" (*Most* everyone has gone.)	1		.36	
Double negative (I did*n't* want to go for *no* more rides.)	1		.36	
		15		5.36

APPENDIX B

TABLE 3 (*Continued*)

SUBJECT — VERB DISAGREEMENT

Error	No. Errors	%
"There" Vs — Npl (There *is* no *noises.*)	5	1.79
Singular collective N — Vpl (A football *team consist* of eleven men.)	2	.71
Plural collective N — Vs (Modern *times has* made this...)	1	.36
Ns (P-grp pl)^m — Vpl (The *size* of the mats *are* the same.)	1	.36
Ns (P-grp S-grp s) — Vpl + Npl (The next *part* of the body that is important to the player *are* his hands.)	1	.36
"Each" (P-grp) — Vpl (*Each* of the foregoing *are* things ...)	1	.36
"Some" (P-grp S-grp s) — Vs (*Some* of the things that are advantageous to a good player *is* ...)	1	.36
Npl (P-grp pl) — Vs (The *walls* on the inside of the rooms *is* ...)	1	.36
Npl — Vs (Agricultural and allied *business has* increased.)	1	.36
	14	5.00

^m "s" or "pl" following P-grp or S-grp means that the last word in that group is singular or plural.

FAULTY COMPARISONS

Error	No. Errors			%	
"More/-er ... than"					
Incomplete (They would get *more* enjoyment.)	4				
Incorrect pronoun case (I found myself with boys younger than *me.*)	1				
		5		1.79	
"as ... as"					
Intrusive "if not better" (I could run as well, *if not better,* than the others.)	2				
Incomplete (They would live twice *as* long.)	1				
		3		1.07	
"the other[s]" (Each branch of service tries to outdo the *other.*)		2		.71	
Omission of *-est* (So I came expecting the *worse* of everything.)		2		.71	
Carelessness (The *big* the hands the more control a person has.)		1		.36	
			13		4.64

TABLE 3 (*Continued*)

A — AN

Error		No. Errors		%
Omission of -n (He is *a* immature individual.)			5	1.79
			280	100.00

BIBLIOGRAPHY

Arnold, H. J., "Diagnostic and Remedial Techniques for College Freshmen", *Association of American Colleges Bulletin*, 16 (1930), pp. 262-279.

Blair, Glenn Myers, *Diagnostic and Remedial Teaching in Secondary Schools* (New York, The Macmillan Co., 1946).

Brueckner, Leo J., and Melby, Ernest O., *Diagnostic and Remedial Teaching* (Boston, Houghton Mifflin Co., 1931).

Charters, W. W., and Miller, Edith, "A Course of Study in Grammar", *University of Missouri Bulletin*, Vol. 16, #2. Education Series 9 (Columbia, Missouri, University of Missouri, January, 1915).

Dunlap, Knight, *Habits. Their Making and Unmaking* (New York, Liveright, Inc., 1932).

The English Language Arts in the Secondary School, The Commission on the English Curriculum of the National Council of Teachers of English (New York, Appleton-Century-Crofts, Inc., 1956).

English Language Institute Staff, *English Sentence Patterns* (Ann Arbor, University of Michigan Press, 1960).

Francis, W. Nelson, *The Structure of American English* (New York, The Ronald Press Co., 1958).

Fries, Charles Carpenter, *American English Grammar* (New York, D. Appleton-Century Co., 1940).

——, *The Structure of English* (New York, Harcourt, Brace and Co., 1952).

——, *Teaching and Learning English as a Foreign Language* (Ann Arbor, University of Michigan Press, 1945).

——, *The Teaching of the English Language* (New York, Thomas Nelson and Sons, 1927).

Gladfelter, M. E., "Values of the Cooperative English Test in Prediction for Success in College", *School and Society*, 44 (September, 1936), pp. 383-384.

Gleason, H. A., Jr., *An Introduction to Descriptive Linguistics* (New York, Holt, Rinehart and Winston, 1961).

"Has English Zero Seen Its Day? — A Symposium", *College Composition and Communication*, VIII (May, 1957), pp. 72-95.

Hollingworth, H. L., *The Psychology of Thought* (New York, D. Appleton-Century Co., 1926).

James, William, *The Principles of Psychology*, Vol. I (New York, Henry Holt and Co., 1890).

——, *Talks to Teachers on Psychology* (New York, Henry Holt and Co., 1939).

Jespersen, Otto, *How to Teach a Foreign Language*, Translated by Sophia Yhlen-Olsen Bertelsen (London, S. Sonnenschein and Co., Ltd., 1904).

——, *The Philosophy of Grammar* (London, George Allen and Unwin, Ltd., 1924).

Kierzek, John M., *The Macmillan Handbook of English*, 3d ed. (New York, The Macmillan Co., 1954).

Lado, Robert, "Sentence Structure", *College Composition and Communication*, VIII (February, 1957), pp. 14-15.

Leonard, Sterling A., *Current English Usage* (= *National Council of Teachers of English Monographs*, 1) (Chicago, The Inland Press, 1932).

Lloyd, Donald J., and Warfel, Harry R., *American English in Its Cultural Setting* (New York, Alfred A. Knopf, 1957).

Lyman, Rollo L., *Summary of Investigations Relating to Grammar, Language, and Composition* (Supplementary Educational Monographs) (Chicago, University of Chicago, 1929).

Marckwardt, Albert H., and Walcott, Fred G., *Facts About Current English Usage* (New York, D. Appleton-Century Co., 1938).

Palmer, Harold E., *The Oral Method of Teaching Languages* (Cambridge, W. Heffer and Sons, Ltd. 1955).

——, *The Principles of Language Study* (London, George G. Harrap and Co., Ltd., 1921).

Pooley, Robert C., *Teaching English Usage* (New York, D. Appleton-Century Co., Inc., 1946).

Pressey, S. L., "A Statistical Study of Children's Errors in Sentence Structure", *English Journal*, 14 (September, 1925), pp. 529-535.

Shupe, Eldon E., Jr., "An Evaluation of Remedial English at Flint Junior College, 1957-1958", Unpublished Ed. D. in English dissertation, University of Michigan (1959).

Stormzand, Martin J., and O'Shea, M. V., *How Much English Grammar?* (Baltimore, Warwick and York, Inc., 1924).

JANUA LINGUARUM

STUDIA MEMORIAE NICOLAI VAN WIJK DEDICATA

Edited by C. H. van Schooneveld

SERIES PRACTICA

1. MARILYN CONWELL and ALPHONSE JUILLAND: Louisiana French Grammar, I: Phonology, Morphology, and Syntax. 1963. 207 pp., 2 maps. Cloth.   Gld. 36.—

3. IRENE GARBELL: The Jewish Neo-Aramaic Dialects of Persian Azerbaijan: Linguistic Analysis and Folkloristic Texts. 1965. 342 pp., map. Cloth.   Gld. 64.—

4. MORRIS F. GOODMAN: A Comparative Study of Creole French Dialects. 1964. 143 pp., map.   Gld. 22.—

5. ROLAND HARWEG: Kompositum und Katalysationstext, vornehmlich im späten Sanskrit. 1964. 164 pp.   Gld. 25.—

6. GUSTAV HERDAN: The Structuralistic Approach to Chinese Grammar and Vocabulary: Two Essays. 1964. 56 pp., 4 figs.   Gld. 18.—

7. ALPHONSE JUILLAND: Dictionnaire Inverse de la Langue Française. 1965. 564 pp., 9 figs. Cloth.   Gld. 80.—

8. A. HOOD ROBERTS: A Statistical Linguistic Analysis of American English. 1965. 437 pp., 11 figs., 6 tables. Cloth.   Gld. 54.—

9. VALDIS LEJNIEKS: Morphosyntax of the Homeric Greek Verb. 1964. 92 pp.   Gld. 15.—

10. ROBERT E. DIAMOND: The Diction of the Anglo-Saxon Metrical Psalms. 1963. 59 pp.   Gld. 10.—

11. JOSEPH E. GRIMES: Huichol Syntax. 1964. 105 pp.   Gld. 18.—

12. CLARA N. BUSH: Phonetic Variation and Acoustic Distinctive Features: A Study of Four General American Fricatives. 1964. 161 pp., 64 figs., 84 tables.   Gld. 30.50

13. WILLIAM E. CASTLE: The Effect of Selective Narrow-Band Filtering on the Perception of Certain English Vowels. 1964. 209 pp., 53 figs., 84 tables.   Gld. 38.—

14. ANN SHANNON: A Descriptive Syntax of the Parker Manuscript of the Anglo-Saxon Chronicle from 734-891. 1964. 68 pp.   Gld. 13.—

15. EICHI KOBAYASHI: The Verb Forms of the *South English Legendary*. 1964. 87 pp.   Gld. 17.—

16. HOMER L. FIRESTONE: Description and Classification of Sirionó, a Tupí-Guaraní Language. 1965. 70 pp., 7 figs.   Gld. 18.—

17. WOLF LESLAU: Ethiopian Argots. 1964. 65 pp.   Gld. 16.—

19. EUGENE A. NIDA: A Synopsis of English Syntax. Second, revised edition. 1966. 180 pp.   Gld. 21.—

21. ERICA REINER: A Linguistic Analysis of Akkadian. 1966. 155 pp., graph.   Gld. 30.—

23. MARVIN K. MAYERS (ed.), Languages of Guatemala. 1966. 318 pp.   Gld. 40.—

MOUTON & CO · PUBLISHERS · THE HAGUE